Towards Digital Language Equality Workshop (TDLE 2022)

Held at LREC 2022

Marseille, France
20 – 25 June 2022

Editors:

Itziar Aldabe
Begona Altuna
Aritz Farwell
German Rigau

ISBN: 978-1-7138-6141-6

Printed from e-media with permission by:

Curran Associates, Inc.
57 Morehouse Lane
Red Hook, NY 12571

Some format issues inherent in the e-media version may also appear in this print version.

Association for Computational Linguistics
209 N. Eighth Street
Stroudsburg, Pennsylvania 18360

Phone: 1-570-476-8006
Fax: 1-570-476-0860

acl@aclweb.org

Additional copies of this publication are available from:

Curran Associates, Inc.
57 Morehouse Lane
Red Hook, NY 12571 USA
Phone: 845-758-0400
Fax: 845-758-2633
Email: curran@proceedings.com
Web: www.proceedings.com

LREC 2022 Workshop
Language Resources and Evaluation Conference
20-25 June 2022

Towards Digital Language Equality Workshop (TDLE)

PROCEEDINGS

Editors:
Itziar Aldabe, Begoña Altuna, Aritz Farwell, German Rigau

Proceedings of the LREC 2022 workshop Towards Digital Language Equality (TDLE 2022)

Edited by:
Itziar Aldabe, Begoña Altuna, Aritz Farwell, German Rigau

For more information:
European Language Resources Association (ELRA)
9 rue des Cordelières
75013, Paris
France
http://www.elra.info
Email: lrec@elda.org

Preface

This volume documents the Proceedings of the Workshop Towards Digital Language Equality (TDLE), held on 20 June, 2022 as part of the LREC 2022 conference (International Conference on Language Resources and Evaluation).

Language Technology (LT), one of the most important applications of Artificial Intelligence, is revolutionizing many language-related tasks while engendering a rapidly growing and substantial economic impact. Although cross-language communication forms a significant part of this development, LT resources are not equally available to all languages and domains. To make use of Language Technology's full potential, progress towards a multilingual, efficient, accurate, explainable, ethical, fair and unbiased language understanding is necessary – in short: Digital Language Equality (DLE).

The workshop at LREC brought together researchers and scholars working on policies, initiatives, projects, and research that target DLE at every administrative level. These include models and tools that monitor, measure, catalogue or visualize the evolution and dynamics of DLE through technological factors, (e.g., the available language resources, tools and technologies) and contextual factors (e.g., societal, economic, educational, industrial).

We are thankful to the authors who submitted their work to this workshop. In the end, six papers were accepted. We are also grateful to our Program Committee members and reviewers for their contributions, to Antonios Anastasopoulos who kindly accepted to be our invited speaker and gave a talk on "Measuring Cultural Representativeness and Rethinking LT4All", and to the LREC committee for accepting this workshop as part of LREC 2022.

Organizers

Itziar Aldabe (HiTZ, UPV-EHU)
Begoña Altuna (HiTZ, UPV-EHU)
Aritz Farwell (HiTZ, UPV-EHU)
Federico Gaspari (ADAPT, DCU)
Maria Giagkou (Athena RC/ILSP)
Jan Hajic (Charles University)
Stelios Piperidis (Athena RC/ILSP)
Georg Rehm (DFKI)
German Rigau (HiTZ, UPV-EHU)
Andy Way (ADAPT, DCU)

Program Committee:

Xabier Arregi (HiTZ, UPV/EHU)
Dimitra Anastasiou (Luxembourg Institute of Science and Technology)
Albina Auksoriute (LIETUVIU KALBOS INSTITUTAS)
Jeremy Barnes (HiTZ, UPV/EHU)
Khalid Choukri (ELDA)
Bessie Dendrinos (ECSPM)
Itziar Gonzalez-Dios (HiTZ, UPV/EHU)
Kristine Eide (Language Council of Norway)
Ainara Estarrona (HiTZ, UPV/EHU)
Inma Hernáez (HiTZ, UPV/EHU)
Jaroslava Hlaváčová (CUNI)
Mikel Iruskieta (HiTZ, UPV/EHU)
Sabine Kirchmeier (EFNIL)
Svetla Koeva (INSTITUTE FOR BULGARIAN LANGUAGE)
Krister Linden (UH)
Teresa Lynn (DCU)
Maite Melero (BSC)
Eva Navas (HiTZ, UPV/EHU)
Delyth Prys (BU)
Kepa Sarasola (HiTZ, UPV/EHU)
Claudia Soria (ELEN)
Frieda Steurs (Instituut voor de Nederlandse Taal)
Jana Straková (CUNI)
Tamás Váradi (Nyelvtudományi Kutatóközpont)
Francois Yvon (CNRS)

Table of Contents

Conference Program

14:00–14:45 *Measuring Cultural Representativeness and Rethinking LT4All*
Antonios Anastasopoulos

14:50–15:20 *Developing an agenda and a roadmap for achieving full digital language equality in Europe by 2030*

15:20–15:40 *Introducing the Digital Language Equality Metric: Technological Factors*
Federico Gaspari, Owen Gallagher, Georg Rehm, Maria Giagkou, Stelios Piperidis, Jane Dunne and Andy Way

15:40–16:00 *Introducing the Digital Language Equality Metric: Contextual Factors*
Annika Grützner-Zahn and Georg Rehm

16:30–16:50 *Collaborative Metadata Aggregation and Curation in Support of Digital Language Equality Monitoring*
Maria Giagkou, Stelios Piperidis, Penny Labropoulou, Miltos Deligiannis, Athanasia Kolovou and Leon Voukoutis

16:50–17:10 *Measuring HLT Research Equality of European Languages*
Gorka Artola and German Rigau

17:10–17:30 *National Language Technology Platform for Public Administration*
Marko Tadić, Daša Farkaš, Matea Filko, Artūrs Vasiļevskis, Andrejs Vasiļjevs, Jānis Ziediņš, Željka Motika, Mark Fishel, Hrafn Loftsson, Jón Guðnason, Claudia Borg, Keith Cortis, Judie Attard and Donatienne Spiteri

17:30–17:50 *The Nós Project: Opening routes for the Galician language in the field of language technologies*
Iria de-Dios-Flores, Carmen Magariños, Adina Ioana Vladu, John E. Ortega, José Ramom Pichel, Marcos García, Pablo Gamallo, Elisa Fernández Rei, Alberto Bugarín-Diz, Manuel González González, Senén Barro and Xosé Luis Regueira

Proceedings of the TDLE Workshop @LREC2022, pages 1–12
Marseille, 20 June 2022

Introducing the Digital Language Equality Metric: Technological Factors

Federico Gaspari[1], Owen Gallagher[1], Georg Rehm[2], Maria Giagkou[3], Stelios Piperidis[3], Jane Dunne[1], Andy Way[1]
[1]ADAPT Centre, School of Computing, Dublin City University, Ireland
[2]Deutsches Forschungszentrum für Künstliche Intelligenz GmbH (DFKI), Germany
[3]Institute for Language and Speech Processing, Research Centre "Athena", Greece
{firstname.lastname}@adaptcentre.ie, {firstname.lastname}@dfki.de, {mgiagkou, spip}@athenarc.gr

Abstract

This paper introduces the concept of Digital Language Equality (DLE) developed by the EU-funded European Language Equality (ELE) project, and describes the associated DLE Metric with a focus on its technological factors (TFs), which are complemented by situational contextual factors. This work aims at objectively describing the level of technological support of all European languages and lays the foundation to implement a large-scale EU-wide programme to ensure that these languages can continue to exist and prosper in the digital age, to serve the present and future needs of their speakers. The paper situates this ongoing work with a strong European focus in the broader context of related efforts, and explains how the DLE Metric can help track the progress towards DLE for all languages of Europe, focusing in particular on the role played by the TFs. These are derived from the European Language Grid (ELG) Catalogue, that provides the empirical basis to measure the level of digital readiness of all European languages. The DLE Metric scores can be consulted through an online interactive dashboard to show the level of technological support of each European language and track the overall progress toward DLE.

Keywords: Digital Language Equality, Technological Factors, Language Resources, Tools, Technologies, Europe

1 Introduction and Background

1.1 Motivation and Objectives

In a plenary meeting on 11 September 2018, the European Parliament adopted by an overwhelming majority a joint ITRE/CULT report, *Language equality in the digital age*, with a resolution that included over 40 recommendations. These concerned *inter alia* the enhancement of the institutional framework for Language Technology (LT) policies at EU level, as well as of EU research and education policies to improve the future of LTs in Europe, so that all stakeholders could benefit from them (European Parliament, 2018).

In an effort to address these recommendations, the European Language Equality (ELE) project[1] (Rehm et al., 2022; Rehm and Way, 2022) with its 52-member consortium is engaged in responding to the call to establish a much-needed large-scale, long-term coordinated funding programme for research, development and innovation in the field of LTs, at European, national and regional levels, designed to meet Europe's needs and demands. By addressing some of the key recommendations issued by the European Parliament, ELE is laying the foundation to draw up an evidence-based Strategic Research, Innovation and Implementation Agenda (SRIA) and Roadmap with strong support from the wider community, as a basis to launch a large-scale programme to achieve full Digital Language Equality (DLE) in Europe by 2030.

The ELE consortium is ideally positioned to pursue this ambitious objective, in that its members include a combination of research and academic organisations, networks, associations and initiatives as well as companies from all over Europe. In addition to all official European languages, the partners' combined expertise covers a very wide range of regional and minority languages, either through consortium partners or through several umbrella organisations.

[1]https://european-language-equality.eu

1.2 Current Situation and Related Work

While the ongoing work conducted by ELE is focused on the languages of Europe, it is situated in a broader context of recent similar efforts with a wider remit. Joshi et al. (2020) investigate the relation between the languages of the world and the resources available for them as well as their coverage in Natural Language Processing (NLP) conferences, providing evidence for the severe disparity that exists across languages in terms of technological support and attention paid by academic, scientific and corporate circles.

Blasi et al. (2021) argue that the substantial progress brought about by the generally improved performance of NLP methods "has been restricted to a minuscule subset of the world's 6,500 languages", and present a framework for gauging the global utility of LTs in relation to demand, based on the analysis of a sample of over 60,000 papers from all major international NLP conferences. This study also shows convincing evidence for the striking inequality in the development of LTs across the world's languages. While this severe imbalance is partly in favour of a few, mostly European, languages, on the whole most European languages are at a disadvantage. Acknowledging that LTs are generally becoming increasingly ubiquitous, Faisal et al. (2021) look into the efforts to expand the language diversity and coverage of NLP applications. Since a key factor determining the quality of present-day NLP systems is data availability, they study the geographical representativeness of language datasets, to assess the extent to which they match the needs of the members of the respective language communities, with a thorough analysis of the striking inequalities.

Bromham et al. (2021) examine the effects of a wide range of demographic and socio-economic aspects on the use and status of the languages of the world, and reach the conclusion that language diversity is under threat across the globe, including in industrialised and economically advanced regions. In particular, this study found that half of the languages under investigation face serious risks of extinction, potentially within a generation, if not imminently. This is certainly a very sombre situation to face up to, which calls for a large-scale mobilisation of all possible efforts by all interested parties to avoid such a daunting prospect, especially for the languages addressed by ELE.[2] It should be emphasised that ELE covers not only the official languages of the European Union or national languages, but also regional and minority languages, and in fact these receive special attention insofar as they are among the least resourced and those with more limited technological support, which puts their communities at a serious disadvantage in the digital age.

1.3 Structure of the Paper

The rest of this article is organised as follows. Section 2 explains the principles behind the Digital Language Equality concept adopted in ELE and the rationale for the DLE Metric with an emphasis on the Technological Factors (TFs). Section 3 zooms in on the TFs, which are complemented by the Contextual Factors (CFs), outlining their main components and discussing the role of the European Language Grid (ELG) as its empirical evidence. The weights assigned to the feature values of the TFs are described, reporting on the main findings of the experiments that were conducted to refine the first implementation of the DLE Metric. The discussion emphasises the flexibility of the DLE Metric, that can be adapted in the future to accommodate subsequent developments and novelties in the community that it may not be possible to anticipate at present. We present our initial results regarding the current level of technological support and digital readiness of Europe's languages based on the TFs of the DLE Metric (the Technological DLE score), computed using a weighting scheme. We also briefly review some of the main open issues and challenges that remain to be addressed. Finally, Section 4 draws some conclusions, pointing out the value and potential of the DLE Metric to benefit the wider LT community and, ultimately, the European citizens on the whole by supporting their future aspirations in the digital age.

[2] https://european-language-equality.eu/languages/

2 Digital Language Equality Metric

2.1 Guiding Principles

This paper introduces the notion of Digital Language Equality (DLE) developed in the project ELE to pursue its ambitious objectives, and presents the associated metric, focusing in particular on the Technological Factors (TFs). The DLE definition is intended to serve the needs of the languages in scope of ELE and the expectations of the relevant language communities in the future. It should be noted that language "equality" does not mean "sameness" on all counts, regardless of the respective environments; we recognise the different historical developments and current situations of the very diverse languages targeted in and by the project, along with their specific features, different needs and realities of their communities, e. g., in terms of number of speakers, ranges of use, etc., which inevitably vary significantly. It would be naive and unrealistic in practice to ignore these facts, and to set out to erase the differences that make languages truly unique, as key components of the heritage and as a vital reflection of the communities that use them. This is also a core element of multilingualism in Europe, where all languages are valued as inherent components of the social fabric that connects European citizens in their diversity. The situational context in which the languages are used, which includes societal, economic, educational, and industrial aspects, is incorporated in the DLE definion and metric through the Contextual Factors (CFs), which complement the TFs and are the subject of a companion paper (Grützner-Zahn and Rehm, 2022).

The notion of DLE promoted by ELE does not involve any judgement of the political, social and cultural status or value of the languages, insofar as they collectively contribute to a multilingual Europe, that should be supported and promoted. Alongside the fundamental concept of equality, we also recognise the importance of the notion of equity, meaning that for some languages, and for some needs, a specific effort is necessary. For example, the availability of, and access to, certain services and resources (e. g., to revitalise a language, or to promote the development of education through that language) is very important for some of Europe's languages. With this in mind, the challenge tackled by ELE is to enable all languages of Europe, regardless of their specific circumstances, to realise their full potential, supporting them in achieving full digital equality. The DLE metric, whose TFs are presented here, captures the needs and expectations of the various European languages and the shortfalls with respect to being adequately supported in terms of resources, tools and technological services in the digital age so as to achieve digital language equality.

2.2 Defining the DLE Metric

Following consultations within the ELE consortium, early in the project a definition of DLE was adopted to guide our efforts. The definition of DLE drew inspiration, among others, from the META-NET White Paper Series (Rehm and Uszkoreit, 2012) and from BLARK[3] (Krauwer, 2003), both of which have been used in the past to assess the level of technological support of specific languages. ELE defines DLE as "the state of affairs in which all languages have the technological support and situational context necessary for them to continue to exist and to prosper as living languages in the digital age" (Gaspari et al., 2021; Gaspari et al., 2022). This definition provides the basis to establish a metric that enables the quantification of the level of technological support for each language in scope of ELE with descriptive, diagnostic and predictive value to successfully promote digital language equality. This approach enables comparisons across languages, tracking their advancement towards the goal of DLE, as well as the prioritisation of needs, especially to fill existing gaps, focusing on realistic and feasible targets. The DLE Metric is therefore defined as "a measure that reflects the digital readiness of a language and its contribution to the state of technology-enabled multilingualism, tracking its progress towards the goal of DLE" (Gaspari et al., 2021). The DLE Metric is computed for each language on the basis of various factors, grouped into TFs (e. g., the available language resources, tools and services, which are the focus of this paper) and situational CFs, e. g., societal, economic, educational, industrial, which are described in detail by Grützner-Zahn and Rehm (2022).

2.3 Key Features

The DLE definition and the formulation of the DLE Metric are modular and flexible, i. e., they consist of well-defined separate and independent, but tightly integrated quantifiers, measures and indicators, selected to ensure compatibility and interoperability with the metadata schema adopted by ELE's sibling EU-funded project European Language Grid (ELG)[4] (Labropoulou et al., 2020; Rehm et al., 2020; Rehm, 2022), which plays a crucial technical role with regard to the TFs. ELG maintains a cloud platform that bundles together data sets, corpora, functional software, repositories and applications to benefit European society, industry and academia and administration, while also addressing the fragmentation of the European LT landscape by providing a convenient single access point.

The definitions of DLE and its metric have also been designed to be transparent and similarly intuitive for linguists, LT experts and developers, language activists, advocates of language and human rights, industrial players, policy-makers and European citizens at large, to encourage the widest possible uptake and buy-in. While we wanted them to be founded on solid, widely agreed principles, we also aimed at striking a balance between a methodologically sound and theoretically convincing approach, and a formulation that can be used, among others, to inform future language and LT policies at the local, regional, national and European levels, to guide and prioritise future efforts in the creation, development and improvement of LRs and LTs, with the ultimate goal of achieving DLE in Europe. Through data analytics and visualisation, languages facing similar challenges in this collective endeavour can be grouped together, and requirements can be formulated to support them in remedying the existing gaps and advancing towards full DLE. An analysis of the Technological DLE scores of European languages is presented in Section 3.4.

A crucial feature of the DLE Metric is its dynamic nature, i. e., the fact that its scores can be updated and monitored over time, at regular intervals or whenever one wishes to check the progress or the status of one or more European languages with respect to the goal of achieving DLE. With regard to the TFs, as the ELG Catalogue organically grows over time, the resulting DLE Metric scores will be updated for all European languages, thereby providing an up-to-date and consistent (i. e., comparable) measurement of the level of LT support and provision that each of them has available, also showing where the status is less than ideal or not at the expected level. The DLE Metric can be found, computed dynamically using the data available in the ELG Catalogue, in the ELE/ELG dashboard.[5]

3 Technological Factors

In order to quantify the level of technological support for a language, we consider a set of TFs. Here we briefly describe their main categories, illustrating the breadth and diversity of the LRs and tools that they capture. The first category of TFs includes tools and services that are offered via the web or running in the cloud, but also downloadable tools, source code, etc.; this category encompasses, for example, NLP tools (morphological analysers, part-of-speech taggers, lemmatisers, parsers, etc.); authoring tools (e. g. spelling, grammar and style checkers); services for information retrieval, extraction, and mining, text and speech analytics, machine translation, natural language understanding and generation, speech technologies, conversational systems, etc.

The second category of TFs includes datasets, i. e. corpora or collections of text documents, text segments, audio transcripts, audio and video recordings, etc., monolingual or bi-/multilingual, raw or annotated. It also encompasses language models and computational grammars and lexical and conceptual resources, including resources organised on the basis of lexical or conceptual entries (lexical items, terms, concepts, etc.) with their supplementary information (e. g., grammatical, semantic, statistical information, etc.), such as computational lexica, gazetteers, ontologies, term lists, thesauri, etc.

[3]http://www.blark.org

[4]https://live.european-language-grid.eu

[5]https://live.european-language-grid.eu/catalogue/dashboard

The technological component of the DLE Metric and the resulting Technological DLE score per language are based on the number of LRs available for a given language. Although an essential aspect of a language's digital readiness is the number of available LRs, equally important are the types and features of these LRs, insofar as they indicate how well a language is supported in all different LT areas. To capture such aspects with the DLE metric, in addition to raw counts of available LRs, the following features of LRs have also been taken into account:

- resource type
- resource subclass
- linguality type
- media type covered or supported
- annotation type, where relevant
- domain covered, where relevant
- function/task performed (for tools/services only)
- conditions of use

The values of these features are appropriately weighted to contribute to the resulting Technological DLE score. The weights applied to LR feature values are listed in Tables 1 and 2 in the Appendix and further discussed in Section 3.1.

3.1 Applying Weights to the Factors

The weights are applied to LR feature values, in order to reward the contribution of a LR to DLE with regard to the relevant TFs. This is based on the assumption that some LR features contribute more effectively to achieving DLE than others. Higher weights are assigned to feature values related to (i) more complex technologies, e. g., LTs that employ or support more than one modality, (ii) more "expensive" datasets/tools, in terms of the investment required to build them, (iii) more "open" or freely available datasets and tools, and (iv) additional or broader envisaged applications.

One guiding consideration in developing the DLE Metric, and especially in assigning the weights of the features and their values for the TFs, was to make the fewest possible assumptions about the (preferred) end-uses and actual application scenarios that may be most relevant to users. These inevitably vary widely due to a number of variables that are impossible to establish *a priori*. We therefore refrained from predetermining particular preferred end-uses when proposing the full specification of the DLE Metric, which otherwise would risk it being unsuitable for some end-users and applications. In Tables 1 and 2 in the Appendix we present the TFs of the DLE Metric with their weights; this set-up is subject to revision as more experiments are run within ELE in addition to those reported in Section 3.2 to adjust the weights, so that the Technological DLE scores capture and reflect fairly the actual level of LT support for the ELE languages.

The features and values for the LRs and LTs that make up the TFs are derived from the metadata schema used in the ELG Catalogue (Labropoulou et al., 2020; Rehm et al., 2020); the weights assigned to them are listed in Table 1 and Table 2 in the Appendix for LRs and tools, respectively. Here we briefly review some of the key features of the TFs, focusing on those that can have several values, which are of particular interest because they show the level of detail and granularity of the metadata accompanying the records included in the ELG Catalogue.

A varied feature within LRs is that of "Annotation Type", which has many possible values. For the first implementation of the DLE Metric, we have assigned a constant very small fixed weight, also based on the fact that some LRs can possess several annotation types. A similar consideration applies to the "Domain" feature, which has many possible values for LRs and for tools: in these cases, the weights assigned to "Domain" values in the first instance are fixed and relatively small, again considering that multiple domains can be combined in a single LR or tool. In addition to "Domain", another feature that appears both in LRs and tools is "Conditions of use"; the weights proposed for this feature of the TFs are identical for the corresponding values of "Conditions of use" across datasets and tools. In the case of (much) more restrictive licensing terms, lower weights are assigned than to liberal use conditions, so they contribute (much) less to the Technological DLE score for the LR in question, and therefore to the cumulative DLE Metric score for that language.

3.2 Experiments with ELG

To experiment with different set-ups for the TFs of the DLE Metric, we used the Catalogue of the European Language Grid, which in early 2022 contained approx. 11,500 records, out of which about 75% were datasets and resources (corpora, lexical resources, models and grammars) and the rest were tools and services, covering almost all European languages. These records contain multiple levels of metadata granularity. We consider the current status of the ELG repository to be representative with regard to the current existence of LT resources for Europe's languages, so it is used by ELE as its empirical basis for the computation of the technological DLE score.

The ELG Catalogue includes metadata of both LRs and LTs for all ELE languages. Each resource and tool has several features and associated values, as shown in the Appendix. Each feature was assigned a weight to calculate the Technological DLE score on a per-language basis, comparing the resulting scores of a number of alternative set-ups, considering especially where each language stood in relation to all the others and how their relative positioning changed as a result of assigning different weights to the various feature values. This was an efficient and effective method to gradually refine the set-up of the TFs and propose the implementation of the relevant weights.

The experiments have shown that the global picture of

the DLE Metric scores for the languages targeted by ELE tends not to change dramatically as the weights assigned to the feature values vary. We have experimented both with very moderate and narrow ranges of weights, and with more extreme and differentiated weighting schemes. Since, ultimately, any changes are applied across the board to all LRs and tools included in ELG for all languages, any resulting changes propagate proportionally to the entire set of languages, thus making any dramatic changes rather unlikely, unless one studiously unduly rewards (i. e., games) specific features that are known to disproportionately affect one or more particular languages. It should immediately be clear that this would be a biased and unfair application of the DLE Metric, and should be avoided at all costs.

Our experiments demonstrate that the overall representation of the languages tends to be relatively stable. This is due partly to the sheer amount of features and possible feature values that make up the TFs. As a result, even if one changes the weights, with the exception of minor and local fluctuations, three main phenomena are generally observed: (i) the overall relative positioning of the languages remains largely stable, with a handful of languages standing out with the highest Technological DLE scores (English leading typically over German, Spanish and French, with the second language having roughly half the Technological DLE score of English), the minimally supported languages still displaying very low scores, and a substantial group of evenly distributed languages towards the middle; (ii) clusters of languages with similar LT support according to intuition and expert opinion remain ranked closely together, regardless of the adjustments made to specific weights for individual features and their values; and, finally, (iii) even when two similarly supported languages change relative positions (i. e., language A overtakes language B in terms of Technological DLE score) as a result of adjusting the weights assigned to features and their values, their absolute Technological DLE scores remain very close.

We have also performed focused checks on pairs or small sets of languages spoken by comparable communities and used in similar circumstances, and whose relative status in terms of LT support is well known to the experts. These focused checks have involved, e. g., Basque and Galician, Irish with respect to Welsh, and the dozen local languages of Italy (also with respect to Italian itself), etc. Overall, the general stability and consistency demonstrated by the Technological DLE scores across different set-ups of weight assignments for the various features and their possible values for TFs provides evidence of its validity as an effective tool to guide developments and track progress towards full DLE for all of Europe's languages by 2030.

Table 1 and Table 2 in the Appendix provide the configuration of the weights assigned to the TFs to compute the Technological DLE score. This set-up is subject to adjustments as more experiments are conducted to check any need to refine the weights, in the interest of making the DLE Metric truly representative of the actual level of LT support for European languages. This approach will ensure that the DLE metric optimally captures the real situation and also effectively reflects the needs and aspirations of all of Europe's languages and their communities for the future in the digital age.

3.3 DLE Metric Formula

Based on the above, the steps to calculate the Technological DLE score are as follows:

1. Each LR in the ELG Catalogue (dataset or tool) obtains a score ($Score_{LR}$), which is equal to the sum of the weights of its relevant features. Specifically for features Annotation Type and Domain, instead of simply adding the respective weight, the weight is multiplied by the number of unique feature values possessed by the LR in question.

   Example: Suppose an LR in the ELG catalogue (LR1) has the following features: corpus, annotated, monolingual, with three different annotation types (morphology, syntax, semantics), with text as media type, covering one domain (e. g. finance), with conditions of use research use allowed. Then, using the weights proposed in Tables 1 and 2 in the Appendix, LR1 is assigned the following score:

   $Score_{LR1} = 5 + 1 + 2.5 + (3 * 0.25) + 1 + (1 * 0.3) + 3.5 = 14.05$

2. To compute the Technological DLE score for language X ($TechDLE_{LangX}$), for all LRs that support language X (LR1, LR2, ... LRN), one sums up the $Score_{LR}$ of all LRs that support language X (LR1, LR2, ... LRN), i. e.

   $TechDLE_{LangX} = Score_{LR1} + Score_{LR2} + \ldots + Score_{LRN}$

3.4 ELE Languages: Technological DLE Scores

Based on the weights, the Technological DLE scores of Europe's languages as of mid-May 2022 are presented in Figure 1. To allow for a more fine-grained visual representation, Figures 2 and 3 in the Appendix show the first and the second half of the languages, respectively, using more appropriate scaling of the score ranges.

Not surprisingly, English is by far the most well-resourced language of Europe, leading the way over German and Spanish, that follow with very similar Technological DLE scores, which are roughly half that of English. French is at present the fourth most well-resourced European language. Finnish, Italian and Portuguese follow at some distance, and it is interesting to note that the next cluster of languages that are spoken by sizeable communities in Europe (Polish, Dutch and Swedish), still in the top ten of the overall list of languages, have a Technological DLE score that is roughly six times lower than that of English.

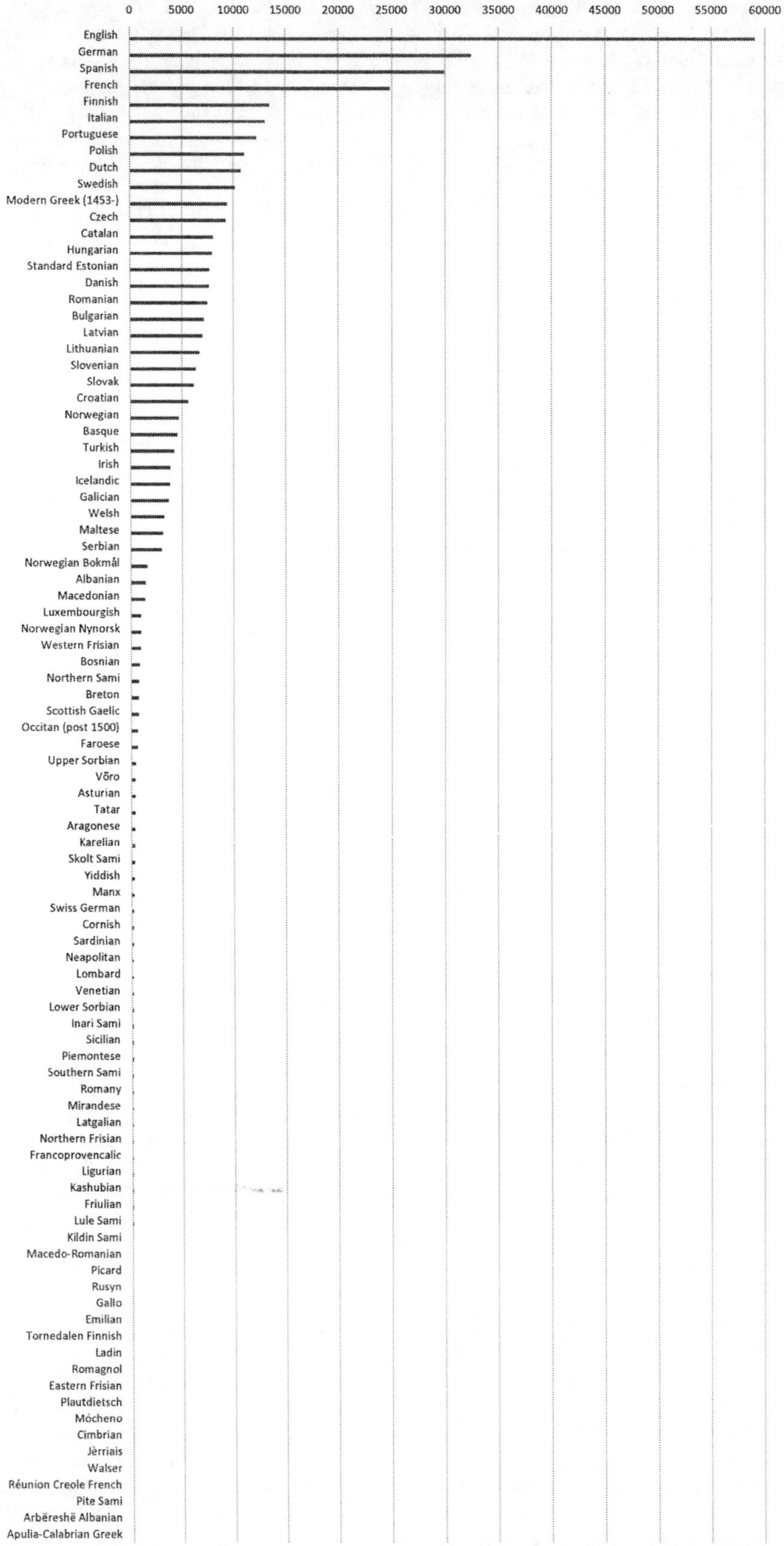

Figure 1: Technological DLE scores for all ELE languages as of mid-May 2022.

A number of observations can be made on the basis of the Technological DLE scores shown in Figures 1, 2 and 3: first, one can see that even some official EU and national languages are not particularly well-supported, at least in comparison with the leading languages, first and foremost English. It should also be noted that some non-official EU languages such as Catalan, Basque, Galician and Welsh appear to be relatively well-supported, also in comparison with some official EU languages. In addition, it is quite striking that several European languages currently represented in ELG have very low Technological DLE scores, which points to the fact that currently most of them have hardly any datasets and basic LTs that are essential for them to remain alive and be used by the respective communities, so as to prosper in the digital area.

3.5 Open Issues and Challenges

The Technological DLE scores discussed here do not take into account the size of LRs or the quality of LRs and LTs. While these are important features, there exist a large variety of size units for LRs, and the way for measuring data size is not standardised, especially for new types of LRs such as models. Regarding the quality of tools in particular, while some information on the Technology Readiness Level scale is available in the ELG Catalogue, the large number of null values does not make it possible to take this aspect into account at the moment. These are shortcomings that we intend to revisit in subsequent efforts, in order to overcome these limitations and improve the overall accuracy and granularity of the Technological DLE score.

As far as datasets are concerned, there could be benefits to setting a minimum size criterion to include LRs such as corpora or grammars in the computation of the Technological DLE score, e. g., to avoid using small resources that cannot be realistically applied in technology development scenarios. However, at present it would be difficult to establish arbitrarily what this minimum size threshold should be, also in recognition of the specifics of the several languages covered by ELE. As a result, the decision was made not to set any minimum size requirement for LRs. The thinking behind this choice was that relatively small data sets are common in less-resourced languages, for particular domains, etc., and there is the possibility to merge small data sets to create bigger ones that would, in fact, be useful, e. g., in domain adaptation for machine translation. More broadly, ELE intends to foster a culture of valuing all and any LRs, especially for less-resourced languages, judiciously balancing the importance given to the size, quantity, diversity and quality of the LRs.

Finally, projects and organisations are not taken into account for the time being, partly due to the difficulty of attributing them specifically to individual languages, even though the possibility remains open to include these additional features and values in the computation of the Technological DLE score at a later stage.

4 Conclusions and Future Work

We introduce the notion of DLE and describe the DLE Metric, focusing in particular on the Technological DLE score, as developed in the ELE project. By providing an empirically-grounded and realistic quantification of the level of technological support possessed by the languages of Europe, the DLE Metric, whose TFs are complemented by the CFs, will contribute to the formulation of the sustainable evidence-based SRIA and Roadmap that will drive future efforts in equipping all European languages with the LTs needed to achieve full DLE in Europe by 2030; the DLE Metric will also provide a transparent means to track and monitor the actual progress in this direction.

With regard to the TFs, the close collaboration with the sister project ELG has been particularly valuable, in that the TFs rely on the metadata in the ELG Catalogue as the ground truth and empirical foundation to measure and quantify the level of digital readiness of the languages covered by ELE. The overview of the TFs is accompanied by an in-depth discussion of the scoring and weighting mechanism adopted for the computation of the Technological DLE score, that is illustrated to explain the overall design of the features and values that contribute to the TFs.

The weights assigned to the features to compute the Technological DLE score can be adjusted going forward. This approach would be useful to address developments ensuing from advances made in LT and as new paradigms or technologies become the state of the art, potentially also as new types of resources emerge and are recognised as crucial for LT support. The ELE consortium views the DLE Metric as a flexible tool, with the possibility of updating and revising if and as needed the exact configuration of the TFs and CFs.

We are confident that the concept of DLE and its associated Metric described here represent valuable tools on which to base subsequent efforts to measure and improve the readiness of Europe's languages for the digital age, also taking into account the situational contexts in which the languages are used via the CFs. By drawing on the descriptive, diagnostic and predictive value of the DLE Metric, the community will have a solid and verifiable means of pursuing and evaluating much-needed developments in the interest of all European citizens. In conclusion, we hope that the DLE Metric will be recognised as a helpful tool by a range of stakeholders at various local, regional, national and European levels who are committed to preventing the extinction of European languages under threat, and who are interested in promoting their prosperity. Such stakeholders include decision- and policy-makers, industry leaders, researchers, developers, and citizens across Europe who will drive forward future developments in the fields of LT and language-centric AI.

Acknowledgements

The work presented in this article was co-financed by the European Union under grant agreement no. LC-01641480 – 101018166. Part of the work has also been supported by the ADAPT Centre for Digital Content Technology which is funded under the Science Foundation Ireland (SFI) Research Centres Programme (Grant No. 13/RC/2106) and is co-funded under the European Regional Development Fund.

5 Bibliographical References

Blasi, D., Anastasopoulos, A., and Neubig, G. (2021). Systematic inequalities in language technology performance across the world's languages. *arXiv*. 2110.06733.

Bromham, L., Dinnage, R., Skirgård, H., Ritchie, A., Cardillo, M., Meakins, F., Greenhill, S. J., and Hua, X. (2021). Global predictors of language endangerment and the future of linguistic diversity. *Nature Ecology & Evolution*.

European Parliament. (2018). Language Equality in the Digital Age. European Parliament resolution of 11 September 2018 on Language Equality in the Digital Age (2018/2028(INI). http://www.europarl.europa.eu/doceo/document/TA-8-2018-0332_EN.pdf.

Faisal, F., Wang, Y., and Anastasopoulos, A. (2021). Dataset geography: Mapping language data to language users. *CoRR*, abs/2112.03497.

Gaspari, F., Way, A., Dunne, J., Rehm, G., Piperidis, S., and Giagkou, M. (2021). D1.1 Digital Language Equality (preliminary definition). https://european-language-equality.eu/wp-content/uploads/2021/05/ELE_Deliverable_D1_1.pdf. Last accessed: 08.02.2022.

Gaspari, F., Grützner-Zahn, A., Rehm, G., Gallagher, O., Giagkou, M., Piperidis, S., and Way, A. (2022). D1.3 Digital Language Equality (full specification of the concept).

Grützner-Zahn, A. and Rehm, G. (2022). Introducing the Digital Language Equality Metric: Contextual Factors. In Itziar Aldabe, et al., editors, *Proceedings of the Workshop Towards Digital Language Equality (TDLE 2022; co-located with LREC 2022)*, Marseille, France.

Joshi, P., Santy, S., Budhiraja, A., Bali, K., and Choudhury, M. (2020). The state and fate of linguistic diversity and inclusion in the NLP world. In *Proceedings of the 58th Annual Meeting of the Association for Computational Linguistics*, pages 6282–6293, Online, July. Association for Computational Linguistics.

Krauwer, S. (2003). The Basic Language Resource Kit (BLARK) as the First Milestone for the Language Resources Roadmap. In *Proceedings of SPECOM 2003*, Moscow, Russia.

Labropoulou, P., Gkirtzou, K., Gavriilidou, M., Deligiannis, M., Galanis, D., Piperidis, S., Rehm, G., Berger, M., Mapelli, V., Rigault, M., Arranz, V., Choukri, K., Backfried, G., Pérez, J. M. G., and Garcia-Silva, A. (2020). Making Metadata Fit for Next Generation Language Technology Platforms: The Metadata Schema of the European Language Grid. In Nicoletta Calzolari, et al., editors, *Proceedings of the 12th Language Resources and Evaluation Conference (LREC 2020)*, pages 3421–3430, Marseille, France. European Language Resources Association (ELRA).

Georg Rehm et al., editors. (2012). *META-NET White Paper Series: Europe's Languages in the Digital Age*, 32 volumes on 31 European languages, Heidelberg etc. Springer.

Georg Rehm et al., editors. (2022). *European Language Equality: A Strategic Agenda for Digital Language Equality*. Cognitive Technologies. Springer. Forthcoming.

Rehm, G., Berger, M., Elsholz, E., Hegele, S., Kintzel, F., Marheinecke, K., Piperidis, S., Deligiannis, M., Galanis, D., Gkirtzou, K., Labropoulou, P., Bontcheva, K., Jones, D., Roberts, I., Hajic, J., Hamrlová, J., Kačena, L., Choukri, K., Arranz, V., Vasiļjevs, A., Anvari, O., Lagzdiņš, A., Meļņika, J., Backfried, G., Dikici, E., Janosik, M., Prinz, K., Prinz, C., Stampler, S., Thomas-Aniola, D., Pérez, J. M. G., Silva, A. G., Berrío, C., Germann, U., Renals, S., and Klejch, O. (2020). European Language Grid: An Overview. In Nicoletta Calzolari, et al., editors, *Proceedings of the 12th Language Resources and Evaluation Conference (LREC 2020)*, pages 3359–3373, Marseille, France. European Language Resources Association (ELRA).

Rehm, G., Gaspari, F., Rigau, G., Giagkou, M., Piperidis, S., Resende, N., Hajic, J., and Way, A. (2022). The European Language Equality Project: Enabling Digital Language Equality for all European Languages by 2030. *EFNIL Conference Publications Cavtat 2021*. 23 pp.

Georg Rehm, editor. (2022). *European Language Grid: A Language Technology Platform for Multilingual Europe*. Cognitive Technologies. Springer. Forthcoming.

Appendix

Feature	Feature Value	Weight
Resource Type	corpus	5
	lexical conceptual resource	1.5
	language description	3.5
Subclass	raw corpus	0.1
	annotated corpus	2.5
	computational lexicon	2
	morphological lexicon	3
	terminological resource	3.5
	Wordnet	4
	Framenet	4
	model	5
	each of the others (there are 15 more)	0.5
Linguality Type	multilingual	5
	bilingual	2
	monolingual	1
Media Type	text	1
	image	3
	video	5
	audio	2.5
	numerical text	1.75
Annotation Type	*each of these – can be combined in a single LR*	0.25
Domain	*each of these – can be combined in a single LR*	0.3
Conditions of Use	other specific restrictions	0.5
	commercial uses not allowed	1
	no conditions	5
	derivatives not allowed	1.5
	redistribution not allowed	2
	research use allowed	3.5

Table 1: Weights assigned to the Technological Factors of the DLE Metric – Language Resources.

Feature	Feature Value	Weight
Language Independent	false	5
	true	1
Input Type	input text	2
	input audio	5
	input image	7.5
	input video	10
	input numerical text	2.5
Output Type	output text	2
	output audio	5
	output video	10
	output image	7.5
	output numerical text	2.5
Function Type	text processing	3
	speech processing	10
	information extraction and information retrieval	7.5
	translation technologies	12
	human-computer interaction	15
	natural language generation	20
	support operation	1
	image/video processing	13
	other	1
	unspecified	1
Domain	*each of these – can be combined in a single tool*	0.5
Conditions of Use	unspecified	0
	other specific restrictions	0.5
	no conditions	5
	commercial uses not allowed	1
	derivatives not allowed	1.5
	redistribution not allowed	2
	research use allowed	3.5

Table 2: Weights assigned to the Technological Factors of the DLE Metric – Tools.

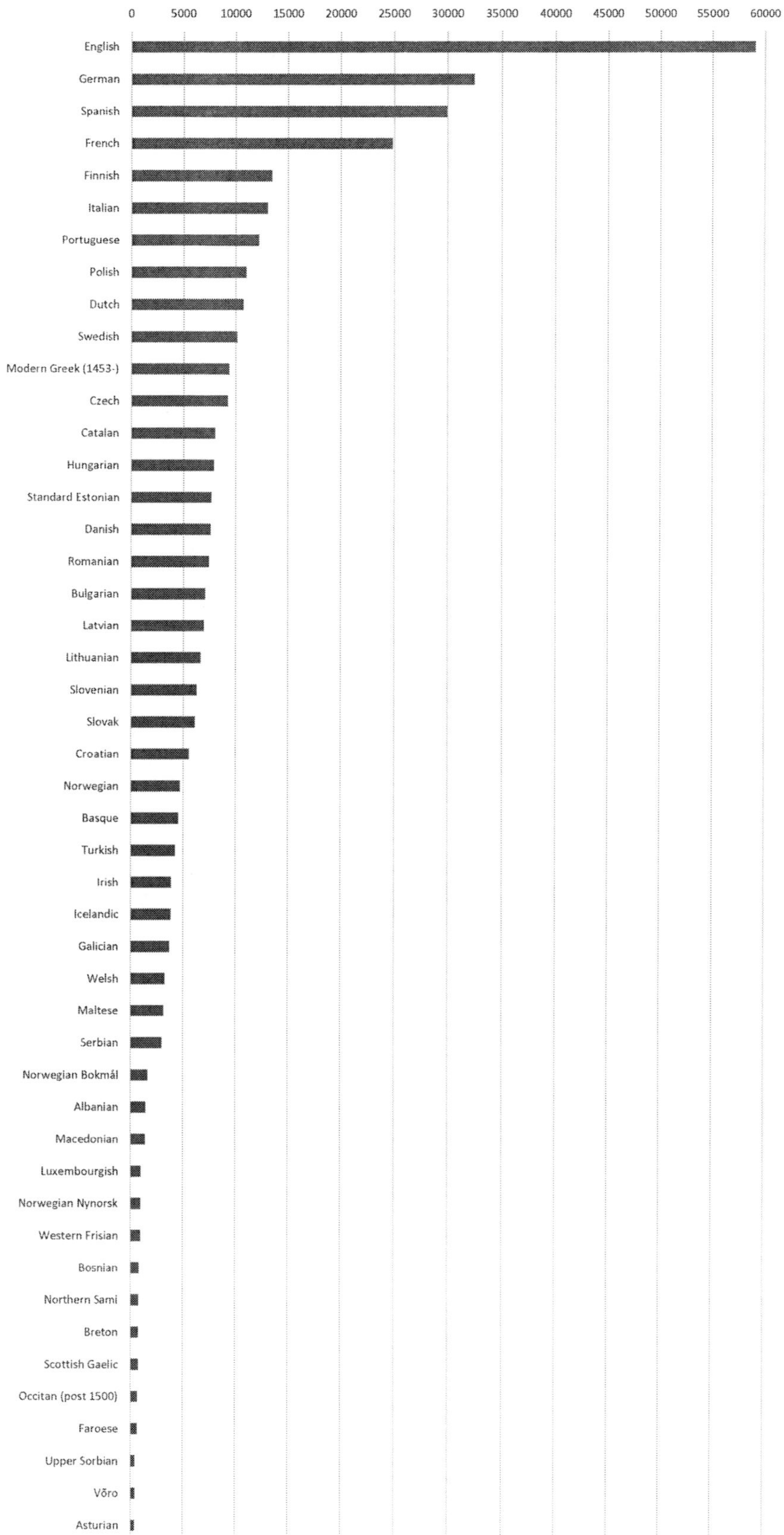

Figure 2: First half of the languages listed in Figure 1 on a range of 0-60,000 Technological DLE score points.

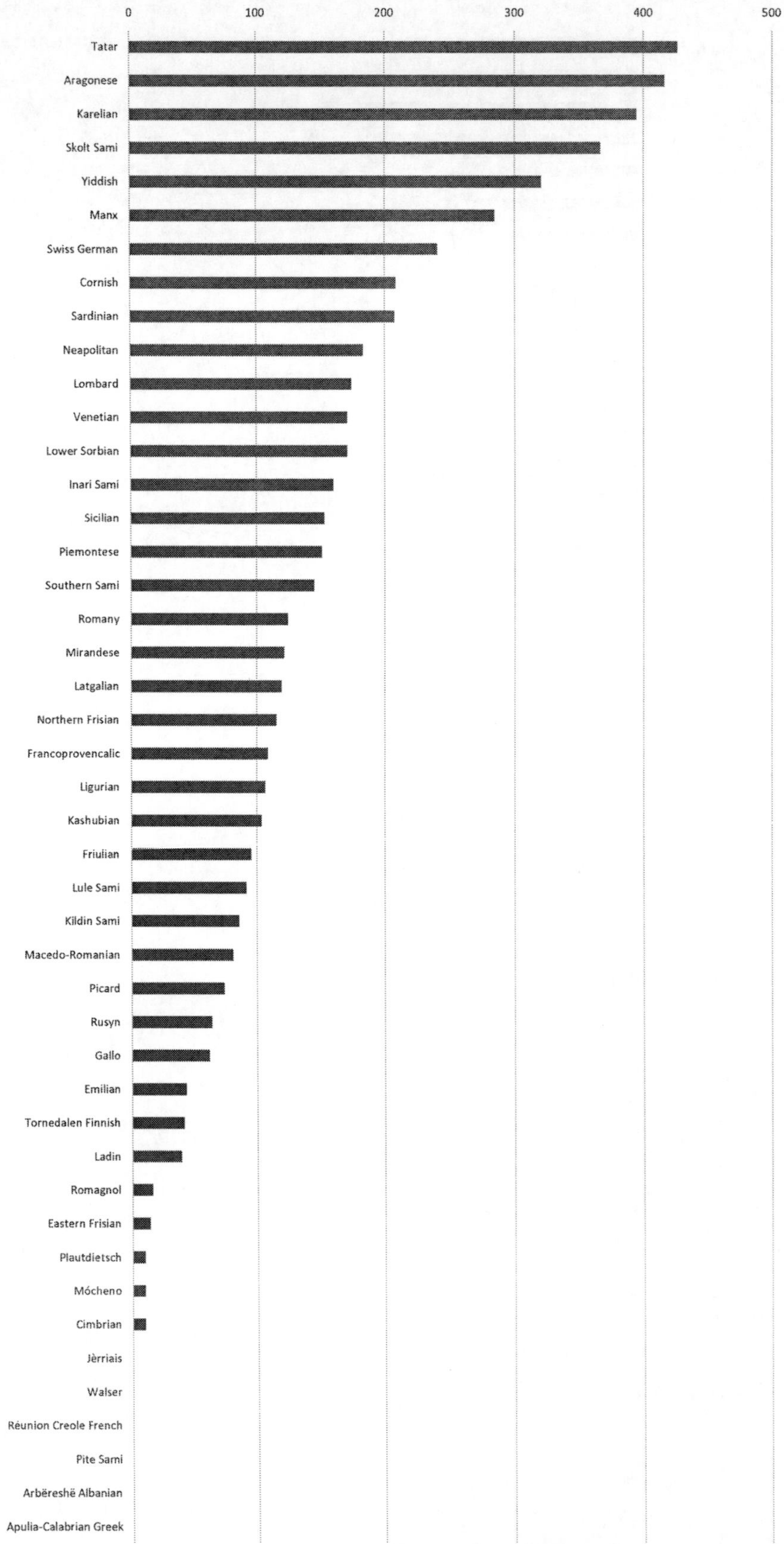

Figure 3: Second half of the languages listed in Figure 1 on a range of 0-500 Technological DLE score points.

Proceedings of the TDLE Workshop @LREC2022, pages 13–26
Marseille, 20 June 2022

Introducing the Digital Language Equality Metric: Contextual Factors

Annika Grützner-Zahn, Georg Rehm
Deutsches Forschungszentrum für Künstliche Intelligenz GmbH (DFKI), Berlin, Germany
{annika.gruetzner-zahn, georg.rehm}@dfki.de

Abstract

In our digital age, digital language equality is an important goal to enable participation in society for all citizens, independent of the language they speak. To assess the current state of play with regard to Europe's languages, we developed, in the project European Language Equality, a metric for digital language equality that consists of two parts, technological and contextual (i. e., non-technological) factors. We present a metric for calculating the contextual factors for over 80 European languages. For each language, a score is calculated that reflects the broader context or socio-economic ecosystem of a language, which has, for a given language, a direct impact for technology and resource development; it is important to note, though, that Language Technologies and Resources related aspects are reflected by the technological factors. To reduce the vast number of potential contextual factors to an adequate number, five different configurations were calculated and evaluated with a panel of experts. The best results were achieved by a configuration in which 12 manually curated factors were included. In the factor selection process, attention was paid to data quality, automatic updatability, inclusion of data from different domains, and a balance between different data types. The evaluation shows that this specific configuration is stable for the official EU languages; while for regional and minority languages, as well as national non-official EU languages, there is room for improvement.

Keywords: Language Technology, Digital Language Equality, Contextual Factors, Europe

1 Introduction

The rising influence of the internet on the daily life impacts the relevance of the automated understanding and production of language in the digital age since natural language is an important part of human-computer-interaction (HCI). From a technological perspective, Language Technologies (LT) can add the "ability to analyze, understand and generate information expressed in natural language" (Aldabe et al., 2021, p. 13) to digital systems. Especially many languages with smaller numbers of speakers are typically under-served in terms of resources and technologies, because of factors as missing economic interest, etc.. To analyse the situation of a language community in the digital sphere, it is necessary to develop a metric which is able to assess the current state of technological support, but that is also able to position the results in the broader socio-economic context of a language and its community. Hence, our suggested Digital Language Equality (DLE) metric consists of two broader groups of factors, *technological* and *contextual* factors.

Especially in multilingual societies, the importance and relevance of DLE is growing every day. In Europe, we are still far away from the ideal situation of DLE which would be "the state of affairs in which all languages have the technological support and situational context necessary for them to continue to exist and to prosper as living languages in the digital age." (Gaspari et al., 2021, p. 4). Back in 2012, the META-NET White Paper Series (Rehm and Uszkoreit, 2012) demonstrated a strong imbalance in terms of technology support for 31 European languages, even though at least the 24 official EU Member State languages have the same status and rights. Additionally, more than 60 regional and minority languages (RML) are protected via the European Charter for Regional or Minority Languages and the Charter of Fundamental rights of the EU (Article 21), which declare the prohibition of discrimination grounded on language (European Union, 1992; European Union, 2010).

The EU-funded project European Language Equality (ELE) addresses the challenge how to solve this existing imbalances. Its main goal is the preparation of a strategic research, innovation and implementation agenda and roadmap that specifies the necessary steps and instruments to achieve DLE in Europe by 2030 (Rehm and Way, 2022). The project covers a total of 89 languages: all 24 official EU languages, 11 official national languages without an official status in the EU and 54 regional and minority languages.[1]

For the preparation of the strategic agenda, the current state of each language needs to be determined as the starting point. In all previous attempts, such as the META-NET White Paper Series, the role of a language's context on the development (or lack thereof) of technologies for that language has been neglected. Accordingly, in this article we focus upon the contextual factors (CF).[2] We prepare different configurations of the metric based on simple classifications of the CFs to assess which factors can and should be included.

Section 2 provides the theoretical background about DLE in Europe and the measurement of the context of languages in the digital world. Section 3 describes the data collection, preparation and calculation of the metric. Section 4 presents the results and evaluation. Section 5 discusses the work and its limitations.

[1] https://european-language-equality.eu/languages/

[2] A complementary paper, Gaspari et al. (2022), focuses on the technological factors.

2 Background and Related Work

2.1 Digital Language Equality in Europe

Digitisation brings people closer together and increases contact across national borders. For interaction across borders to function properly, smooth communication must be possible. However, communication has so far been dominated by a few languages with large communities of speakers or economic dominance. This excludes other language communities and can eventually lead to the digital extinction of a language. To avoid this scenario, smaller languages need to be supported, i. e., DLE must be defined as a societal, political and also scientific goal to enable languages to live and grow in the digital world.

Moreover, a multilingual society without proper translation has consequences. Negative impacts include not knowing certain information due to a lack of information access, no access to digital services in critical domains such as health and e-government, reduced and hindered participation in political processes and differences in cross-border shopping behavior (STOA, 2017; Burchardt et al., 2012; Bali et al., 2019). To avoid these effects, language barriers must be lowered or fully removed. With more than 80 languages in Europe, LTs are the only feasible option.

A recent European Parliament (EP) resolution acknowledges multilingualism to be a property of European diversity. Although it recommends setting up a "large-scale, long-term coordinated funding programme" (European Parliament, 2018) to decrease the differences between the technological support of Europe's languages, an EU policy to challenge language barriers does not exist yet (Aldabe et al., 2021). Additionally, language data, the foundation for the development of LTs, is not classified as "high value data" in the "Directive on open data and the re-use of public sector information", which implies that language data does not provide any benefit to society or economy, which is the main criterion for the classification (European Parliament and Council of the European Union, 2019). This creates an obstacle for LT development.

There are also differences in terms of research on different languages. English is better supported through LTs and is worked upon much more intensively than other languages in published work (Joshi et al., 2020; Blasi et al., 2021; Mager et al., 2018). In Europe, there has been more and more research on languages other than English in the last 10 to 15 years but the overall situation still cannot be considered one of equality.

Krauwer (2003) was one of the first calls for action towards the development of LRs/LTs for under-resourced languages. In the following years, different projects and initiatives established an important resource and technology basis for Europe's languages including, among others, Euromatrix (EU Publications Office, 2017a), FLaReNet (Soria et al., 2012), ITranslate4 (EU Publications Office, 2017b) and CLARIN (Hinrichs and Krauwer, 2014). Additionally, META-NET, an EU Network of Excellence forging the Multilingual Europe Technology Alliance, was established with a group of projects (T4ME, CESAR, METANET4U, META-NORD) promoting and supporting the development of LTs for all European languages (Rehm and Uszkoreit, 2012; Rehm et al., 2014). The EU-funded project CRACKER (Cracking the language Barrier, 2015-2017) continued the work of META-NET, concentrating on additional strategy development and community building. The most recent EU projects in this line of actions are European Language Grid (ELG; Rehm et al., 2020a; Rehm, 2022) and European Language Equality (ELE; Rehm and Way, 2022). ELG and ELE collaborate closely, e. g., the DLE metric, developed in ELE, will be presented in a dedicated dashboard, which will be available in ELG.

In 2017, the report *Language equality in the digital age* was published (STOA, 2017), based on a study conducted by the Scientific Foresight Unit from the European Parliamentary Research Service. This report increased the awareness of the negative impacts of language barriers. LTs were proposed to be a possible answer, but, due to less funding and missing awareness, the danger of digital language extinction still threatens many European languages. Another problem identified was the lack of policies for LTs at national and European level (Rehm et al., 2020b). One year later, the *Language Equality in the digital age* resolution was adopted by the EP, which defines multilingualism as part of our cultural heritage and worthy of protection, as well as a challenge for an inclusive EU. It calls for the legal protection of the 60 European RMLs (European Parliament, 2018).

2.2 Measuring a Language's Context

Recently, research has begun to use data-driven approaches to establish relationships between the technical support of a language and non-technological factors, e. g., by clustering languages according to the number of available LRs and mentions in scientific publications. Joshi et al. (2020) show a correlation between the representation of a language at NLP conferences and the availability of language data. Mentions of each language in conferences were computed using Language Occurrence Entropy. Subsequently, a class-wise Mean Reciprocal Rank calculated the results per class in the conference proceedings.

Blasi et al. (2021) examine the performance of technologies for various languages as well as the correlation of technological and non-technological factors. Leaving technological performance aside, the authors analyse the correlation between the number of citations and the covered language diversity in a paper and between the economic size and number of published papers. A marginal effect was measured between the number of citations and number of languages covered by a paper, i. e., no correlation was detected. Significantly fewer prediction errors were found when the

Gross Domestic Product (GDP) was associated with the number of papers.
Moreover, data sets are also investigated regarding the correlation between geographical or economic factors and the origin of the data set calculating the predictive values for these factors (Faisal et al., 2021).
The AI Vibrancy Tool published with the AI Index report (Stanford University, 2021) computes a score that represents the "AI vibrancy" per country including TFs and non-technological factors. The factors covering research and development are based on numbers about publications, patents, AI conferences and available software. Economy is quantified via numbers about skills, hiring, investment and companies. Inclusion is represented through numbers about women in AI. The measured factors represent the context of AI software development (Zhang et al., 2021a). The calculation consists of the following steps: (1) data normalisation using a scalar; (2) calculation of the arithmetic average per country and indicator; (3) substitution of the values for each country into the formula[3]. Weights are applied to individual scores based on the respective indicator and the area of the indicator. Finally, for each factor a relative score between 0 and 100 is calculated (Stanford University, 2020).
In recent years, first approaches have been made to measure the technical support of languages. But due to the lack of data and the high complexity of the matter, a metric which includes all components is still missing. Section 3 shows that our DLE metric is based on a similar approach as the AI Index meaning it also results in a score through processing a number of factors and it is quantitative and solely data-driven.

3 Method

3.1 Data Collection

The preliminary definition of the DLE metric (Gaspari et al., 2021) included 72 potential contextual factors, clustered into 12 classes representing different aspects of the context of a language. Each of the factors had to be quantified with an indicator to be measurable, which depended on the presence and accessibility of data for a fitting indicator to represent the factor. First, different sources of pan-European data were collected. The selected ones included, among others, EUROSTAT[4], the European Language Monitor[5], Ethnologue[6] and various reports and articles. Second, the data was collected manually for each indicator.
Overall, 27 of the 72 initial factors were excluded due to missing data. This affected especially factors from the classes "research & development & innovation", "society" and "policy". Data about policies is mainly too broad and represents whether policies exist or not. The class "society" included factors about diversity being difficult to quantify. The problem of missing data in this area was already mentioned in the AI Index report (Zhang et al., 2021b). The factors excluded from the class "research & development & innovation" covered mainly figures about the LT research environment, while broader numbers about the research situation of the whole country were indeed available. Table 3 in the Appendix shows all factors from the preliminary definition (Gaspari et al., 2021), their class and the indicator they were quantified with. Overall, 46 factors[7] were quantified with at least one appropriate indicator, some with two indicators representing different perspectives like total numbers and numbers per capita.
The data was collected on 16 of Dec. 2021. Many sources provide their data as Excel sheets. Some data was published on websites. The data for 15 indicators had to be collected manually from reports or articles. We attempt to update the contextual factors on an annual basis. Based on the work presented in this paper, we assume that this process of updating the metric takes approximately one or two weeks.

3.2 Data Preparation

The collected data was very heterogeneous: it had different formats, was based on country or language level, included differing languages or countries and consisted of three data types. Data preparation took several steps, including the standardisation of the format of the numbers, harmonising the names of the languages (Hammarström et al., 2021) and merging the data from different tables. Some sources provided plain text from which a score had to be extracted. Features mentioned in the text were quantified with a score and this score was assigned to countries or language communities. If the text included more than one feature, the scores were added up. For a list of the indicators transformed from plain text and an explanation of the process see Table 4. Because the metric is intended to process data on a language basis, data collected on the country level had to be converted to the language level. In total, the factors were quantified with three different types of data, total numbers, proportional numbers, and scores. Most total numbers were split proportionally, using the percentage of speakers of the language per country. The figures for the percentages were calculated through the population size and the number of speakers from Ethnologue.[8]
Due to some gaps and old records about RMLs, experts on minority languages from the ELE consortium were asked to fill the gaps or to provide better data. The figures for Alsatian, Faroese, Gallo, Icelandic, Macedonian and the Saami languages were corrected.
Percentages of languages often taught as a second language (English, German, French, Spanish) were only included if the language had an official status in the country. For example, the figures for English are based

[3]https://aiindex.stanford.edu/vibrancy/
[4]https://ec.europa.eu/eurostat
[5]http://www.efnil.org/projects/elm
[6]https://www.ethnologue.com
[7]The factor "political activity" was added.
[8]https://european-language-equality.eu/languages/

on the figures of the UK, Ireland and Malta. In other European countries, English does not have an official status, so they were not taken into account. If the language was an official national language in at least one country, only language communities with more than one percent were included to simplify the mapping. This calculation was performed for each language community in each of the European countries covered by the ELE project.

Total numbers per capita, proportional numbers, and scores were applied to the language communities without adjustment due to the complexity and additional time the adaption would have needed. A complex mapping would be desirable, as many language communities deviate from the average. Additionally, the mapping through the proportion of the speakers is problematic, too, because the sum of the speaker communities is not 100% if the country has many bi- or multilingual speakers. Hence, numbers from such countries were given several times. Another problem is the missing inclusion of the political reality regarding the promotion of a language. This refers to figures as to how many researchers work on the language, which were also transferred by a percentage mapping. In countries with a high number of speakers of a language, but less money or activity being spent on the promotion of the language, a direct mapping does not fit.

If a language was spoken in more than one country, total numbers were added up, while proportional numbers, scores and total numbers per capita were calculated through the average. At this point the different sizes of the language communities were slightly taken into account, hence, the data values of bigger language communities were weighted double for the calculation of the average. A complex inclusion of the size of the language community would result in more fine-grained figures and, therefore, probably in different scores.

3.3 Metric Calculation

The data per language community was converted into scores that indicate if a language has a context with the possibility to evolve or not. Without the political will, funding, innovation and economic interest in the region, the probability to achieve DLE is low. In order for the contextual values to be easy to compare and memorise, a score between 0 and 1 was assigned to the languages. Here, 0 represents a context with no potential for the development of LT, while 1 represents the best potential. To keep the metric as transparent as possible, it was decided to base the calculation on an average of the factors. Therefore, the intermediate goal was to calculate a score between 0 and 1 for each factor. The language with the lowest value for the respective factor will be depicted with a 0, the language with the highest value with a 1. The steps were as follows:

1. Calculation of range: highest value - lowest value;
2. $\frac{(value-minimum)*100}{range}$ = Percentage weighting of a language within the range;
3. The result is a relative value: to obtain a score between 0-1 the result is divided by 100;
4. Apply steps 1-3 for all languages and factors;
5. Calculate average of all factors per language;
6. Weighting of the scores with the three factors number of speakers, scores based on the language status and whether the language was an official language of the EU or not.

The three weighting factors were considered to be relevant for the context to develop LTs due to the influence of the number of speakers on the investment by large companies and the legal or EU status on the amount of funding. The weighting included two steps: 1) the calculation of the average of the overall scores, the scores for the number of speakers and the legal status and 2) the addition of 0.07 to the score for each official EU language. The second step was separated from the average calculation, because the indicator consisted of two values, 1 for being and 0 for not being an EU language. Average calculation would result in a too strong boost for the official EU languages. Hence, English had already a score of around 0.7 and 0.8 without the boost, smaller values for EU languages would have penalised English, which would not represent reality.

To create five different versions of the metric, the factors were classified based on the option to update the data automatically and the quality of the data (Table 3, indicators marked with * are automatically updateable and indicators marked with ** provides data with good quality). Data quality was chosen to avoid bias in the outcome of the metric. The possibility to update the data automatically was selected because it would simplify the implementation of the DLE metric in the form of an interactive dashboard in the ELG platform.

Based on these criteria, the following configurations of contextual factors were examined:

1. Factors with available data: 46 factors
2. Factors that can be updated automatically: 34 factors
3. Factors with good data quality: 26 factors
4. Factors that can be updated automatically and that have good data quality: 21 factors
5. Factors were manually curated using four criteria: automatically updatable, good data quality, not more than two factors per class, balance between data types: 12 factors (Table 1 shows the factors included in this configuration)

The fewer factors included in the metric, the more likely it is that an important influencing factor is omitted. However, the risk of distorting the metric with more data is reduced.

Table 1: Factors included in Configuration 5

Class	Factor
Economy	Size of economy
	Size of the ICT sector
Education	Students in LT/language
	Inclusion in education
Industry	Companies developing LTs
Law	Legal status and legal protection
Online	Wikipedia pages
R & D & I	Innovation Capacity
	Number of papers
Society	Size of language community
	Usage of social media
Technology	Digital connectivity, internet access

3.4 Heuristic Expert Evaluation

The results were validated through a heuristic expert evaluation, a method developed by the HCI community to conduct usability analyses. Experts were confronted with an interface and asked to give their opinion. One issue of the method is the lack of reproducibility, as differing opinions between experts produce different results. However, this allows for independent thoughts and maximises the likelihood of discovering aspects not noticed before (Nielsen and Molich, 1990). When three to four experts evaluate an interface together using this method, only 25-50% of errors are detected but with five independent experts between 55 and 90% of errors can be discovered (Georgsson et al., 2014).

We adapted the method for our purposes. The experts did not receive an interface but the results of the five configurations of the metric. The expert panel consisted of ELE consortium partners. The choice of the experts were based on their knowledge in the area of Language Technology, Computational Linguistics, Linguistics, Computer Science and others. Moreover, the experts represent different European countries and know the background of their countries and the languages spoken in the country well. We reached out to 37 (of the, in total, 52) ELE partners from 33 different organisations. The experts were asked to provide an intuitive assessment of the results regarding the languages they know, a feedback explaining how and why they would have expected the results to be and to indicate the most appropriate configuration.

4 Results

4.1 Most Adequate Configuration

The fifth configuration (Figure 1) was evaluated by the experts as being the one that reflects reality most adequately. The results of the other configurations are shown in the Appendix (Figures 2). Overall, the results develop steadily from the first configuration to the fifth in direction of higher scores for the official EU languages and lower scores for the regional and minority languages. From the second to the fifth configuration the results are similar but differ in the score ratios between the language groups (1) official EU languages, (2) national languages but not an official EU language and (3) regional and minority languages.

Diving deeper into the results of the fifth configuration (Figure 1), the calculated scores for the 89 languages with 12 curated factors range between 0.95 and 0. The distinction of 0.05 between the average of 0.14 and the median of 0.09 represents a left shift towards the higher scores. The first third is dominated by the official EU languages (turquoise) ranging between a score of 0.17 and 0.95, while the RMLs (orange) are presented as a long tail with low scores between 0.1 and 0. The official national languages which are not recognised as official EU languages (pink) are between the other two language groups having scores from 0.18 to 0.08. The proximity of English, German and French and the relatively low score for Spanish are caused by the inclusion of only European countries in the data.

Generally, the results exhibit a Northwest to Southeast divide. Usually, the languages spoken in the Northwest of a language group have better scores than the languages spoken in the Southeast of Europe. This tendency materialises especially in the regional and minority languages and less in the official EU languages.

4.2 Heuristic Expert Evaluation

From the 37 contacted partners, 18 provided an assessment of the results. The feedback consisted of overall ratings of the five configurations (Section 4.1) as well as detailed comments regarding individual languages the experts have expertise in. As a consequence, most answers related to official EU languages. RMLs for which feedback was received are spoken in the UK, Spain, Italy and the Nordic countries. We received feedback on 56 of the 89 languages.

In general, using all factors was evaluated as risky due to the possible distortion of results caused by data with bad quality. The results of configuration 1 were indeed considered as being counterintuitive, with high scores for languages as Emilian, Gallo and Franco-Provencial which seemed to be motivated by distorted data. The second configuration was similarly criticised, except for positive comments on the automatic nature of the metric. The results are less distorted but evaluated as worse compared to configurations 3-5. The results of the third and fourth configuration are similar. Focusing on quality data improves the results significantly, but fewer factors eventually imply that relevant important factors for the context may be missing. However, although the factors were reduced the scores remain similar. The fifth configuration was assessed positively regarding the transparency of fewer factors and the possibility to balance the factor classes.

The evaluation of individual languages and their scores showed an improvement from the first configuration with the worst results to the fifth configuration with the best results. Table 2 lists the evaluated languages in

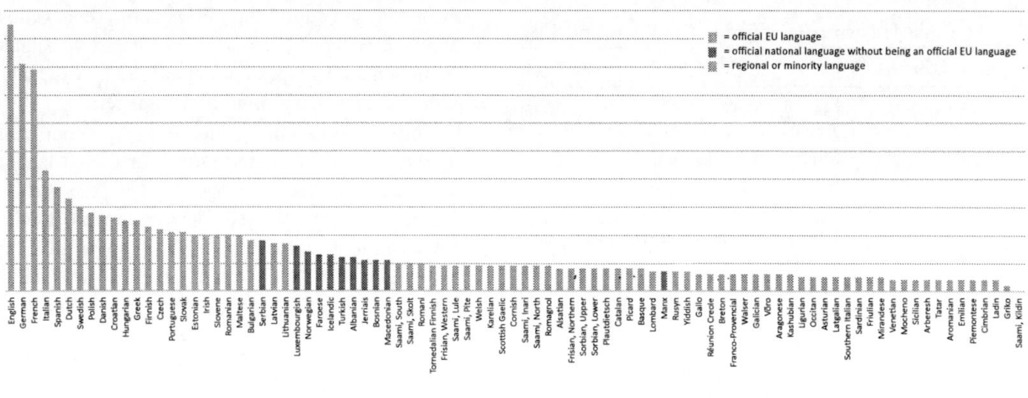

Figure 1: Results of Configuration 5 (12 manually curated factors)

configuration 5 and their assessment by the experts. Overall, the results of the fifth configuration were assessed to represent the context of the language communities in the most adequate way, while there is still room for improvement for a few languages.

Various experts provided suggestions to improve the results, e. g., with regard to the data and data sources. First, it was recommended to collect data in national and regional sources. Additionally, it was pointed out that the context of languages spoken outside of Europe is excluded and therefore important and relevant numbers are missing. Other suggestions refer to missing factors, particularly relevant for RMLs is the inclusion of the vitality status of a language. Another idea was to replace the official EU status as a weighting factor with the respective country's membership in the European Economic Area (EEA), since countries within this alliance have access to European research funds and networks. Moreover, competition between official national languages, as with Irish and English in Ireland, was suggested to be an important factor.

There were also suggestions regarding the presentation of the results. Language communities with complex political backgrounds are most likely to be biased by a rather simplistic calculation based on country data and should be highlighted and presented with the limitations of data-based approaches for such cases. It was also suggested that languages that do not have a writing system are special cases for the development of LTs.

A few experts had more global comments regarding the methodology, which they felt is unable to capture the complex contexts of certain language communities such as Maltese, Irish and the Celtic languages, which scored better than expected. The prosperity of the UK boosts its relevant RMLs with the country-specific data, while in reality these RML communities are strongly dominated by English. The same applies to Ireland and the Irish language. Another point of criticism was the inclusion of data not applied per capita. As a result, small language communities, despite relatively good support, cannot achieve a high score. The size of the language community has an impact on the economic interest, investment, number of researchers, etc. for the language, but for some smaller language communities that have already invested a lot in their language and infrastructure, the score seems too low.

5 Discussion

The DLE metric for the contextual factors has some limitations (see Section 3). First, expanding the data set to include regional or national sources would result in (i) a higher number of factors, (ii) improved data quality, as gaps in individual indicators may be filled, (iii) quantification of more factors with more than one indicator, to reflect different perspectives and (vi) a more complex mapping to language communities based on regional data resulting in a significant impact on RML. Moreover, including the factors suggested by the experts, such as membership in the EEA or language vitality status, could help improve the results.

Second, the data cleaning procedure can be improved. For the calculation of the Innovation Scoreboard (Bielinska-Dusza and Hamerska, 2021), outliers with values outside twice the standard deviation were replaced by the respective maxima or minima of the data series. Data gaps could be filled using data from previous years and skewed data could be corrected using a square root transformation. These steps would most likely affect the results of configurations 1 and 2, since they use the data with poorer quality.

The mapping of country-specific data to language-specific data can be improved, e. g., Bromham et al. (2021) show how a possible regional mapping of data using the World GeoDatasets[9] could be realised. For large countries with bigger regional or urban-rural divides, a regional mapping would represent reality more accurately. In particular, the missing mapping of proportional data, scores and total numbers per capita has a major impact on the results. Here, regional data could help to calculate the average deviation of individual regions or language communities from other proportional data and to transfer this deviation to proportional data

[9]http://worldgeodatasets.com

Suitable	Too high	Too low	Contrary Opinion
English	Irish	Norwegian	French
Dutch	Italian	Spanish	German
Danish	Swedish	Portuguese	Saami, Northern
Polish	Hungarian	Czech	Latvian
Greek	Croatian	Romanian	
Finnish	Maltese	Bulgarian	
Estonian	Faroese	Icelandic	
Slovene	Scottish Gaelic	Emilian	
Slovak	Cornish	Sicilian	
Lithuanian	Manx		
Serbian	Saami, Southern		
Basque	Saami, Pite		
Catalan	Saami, Lule		
Galician	Saami, Skolt		
Asturian	Saami, Inari		
Aragonese	Sardinian		
Welsh	Romagnol		
Griko			
Lombard			
Ligurian			
Venetian			
Southern Italian			
Friulian			
Piemontese			
Ladin			
25	17	9	4

Table 2: Assessment of the individual languages in configuration 5 by the panel of experts

only found on national level, and similarly for the total figures per capita. Another improvement would be to calculate the data merging from the individual language communities in different countries depending on the size of the language community. Currently, the values of larger language communities were double-weighted when determining the average of proportional data, numbers per capita or scores. This simplification could be mitigated by including the total number of speakers per language community in each country. Sustainability was mentioned several times. Romaine (2017, p. 49) stressed the importance of an "on-going monitoring of individual communities" for a reliable evaluation of the situation regarding language diversity which was considered in this approach as an important aspect and taken into account with the inclusion of the criterion automatic updateability of the factors. One problem for the future is the relative calculation from the values to each other. Thus, the scores of *all* languages may change if new values are added, even if the situation of the language community itself has not changed. To mitigate this, a temporal dimension could be integrated (Bielinska-Dusza and Hamerska, 2021). The lowest and highest value of the range for the calculation represent the lowest or the highest value from the last years, which reduces fluctuations.

Another approach would be to measure the prediction accuracy of the CFs with regard to the TFs after some time. In this way, each single factor could be evaluated and unrecognized distortion in the results could be examined and ruled out in the future.

The results show a need for an improvement regarding the context for LT development for all languages except English, French and German. Despite the lack of data about non-European countries with English as the official national language, English achieves the best results in every configuration. Thus, the dominance of English in business and science is reflected in the data. The good results for French and German are grounded in the size of the countries and their economies. Spanish reaches only half the score, even though it has many more speakers. Some experts criticise this result since the context of Spanish for LT development should score higher. As shown by the META-NET White Papers (Rehm and Uszkoreit, 2012), LT support for Spanish is similar to German and French. Since the CFs are supposed to show the achievability of DLE and thus give a 'prediction' for LT development, the results do not fit.

In the META-NET White Paper comparison of the technical support of Europe's languages, the languages that were assessed as having a better technical support in 2012 also perform better in the calculation of the CFs. Always reaching the highest contextual scores, English, Dutch, French, German, Spanish and Italian achieved "moderate support" in at least three of the four LT areas (Rehm and Uszkoreit, 2012). The next set of languages according to the results of the CFs, i. e., Polish, Czech, Swedish, Hungarian and Finnish, also achieved "moderate support" in at least one area in 2012. The fact that these languages achieved better results in 2012 indicates that their context has probably been better ten years ago than for the remaining languages. Greek, Croatian and Danish stand out because these three languages did not reach the "moderate support" level in any of the four groups in 2012. However, since the score for Croatian is considered too high by the experts for all configurations, it can be assumed that the score is distorted by the data. The context for Greek and Danish seems to have improved.

Blasi et al. (2021) and Joshi et al. (2020) highlight the marginal representation in research of languages with a small language community and a low economic weight. The results based on an academic context are not deviating from results based on the entire context as presented in the present paper (Joshi et al., 2020). Additionally, Blasi et al. (2021) point out the more complex the technical task, the worse the technical support languages with a small number of speakers have, i. e., the size of the language community seems to have an influence on the technical support. Faisal et al. (2021) predict the correlation between data sets and the country of origin with three factors: GDP, size of the language community and geographic proximity. Most of the data sets came from economically prosperous countries, thus the best predictive value was the GDP. Additionally, Blasi et al. (2021) show that the GDP has a better predictive power regarding the publication of papers than the number of speakers of a language. According to these results, the GDP has a stronger influence in academia than the size of the language community. However, if language communities have both, a low GDP and few speakers, special effort and support are needed to ensure technical support.

According to the Northwest to Southeast divide identified, it is the context of language communities in the East and South of Europe that needs to be strengthened to achieve DLE. In the META-NET White Paper Series, only three languages spoken in Eastern Europe achieved "moderate support" once in the four areas. In comparison, the technical support of nine languages spoken in the West was rated as "moderate" at least once. Since no other related studies exist, these results can only be discussed in a broader context. For example, Bargaoanu et al. (2019) identified an East-West difference in Europe using data on economic and social development patterns. Although fewer factors were examined, the same pattern emerges. The difference between Northwest and Southeast needs to be reduced to enable all language communities to participate in the digital society. The results are particularly poor for small language communities. In order for the EU to be a truly equal association of countries and language communities, the differences must be evened out. Otherwise, the impact of language barriers (Section 2.1) will remain and even reinforce inequalities.

The results of the CFs along with the technological scores form the Digital Language Equality metric. Both scores will be presented in an interactive, web-based dashboard and will provide information about the current state of LT support based on the TFs and about the situation of the language communities regarding the further development. Together, TF and CF scores/results can be used as the basis for strategic recommendations regarding the future development of languages in the digital world. A language that is poorly supported technologically and has a bad contextual score is unlikely to exhibit significant improvement regarding LT support without changing its context. A language lacking LT support but with a better situational context could indeed take the next steps towards DLE in the coming years. Currently well-supported languages will continue to do well if their good situational context stays intact, while languages with a good technological score and a rather low context, are likely to stagnate technologically.

6 Conclusion

We present a first approach for the calculation of a score, which is meant to reflect the context of a language with respect to the development of LTs. The DLE metric consists of technological factors representing the current state of technical support and contextual factors describing the situation for LT development and achievability of DLE, especially with regard to the languages covered by ELE. The scores can also be used to create initial predictions about the further LT development if the context does not change.

Our initial methodological approach exhibits room for improvement. This applies in particular to the data collection and preparation. The mapping of data from the country to the language level can be improved, reducing inherent inaccuracies affecting data from language communities with few speakers. Another approach could be the calculation of predictive values for individual CFs based on TF scores. This would allow each individual factor to be tested for its predictive power regarding LT development.

The results of the five tested configurations show a clear pattern once they are reduced by the factors that distort the results due poor data quality. There exists a greater difference between the scores of the official EU languages and RMLs, as well as a gradient from Northwest to Southeast within the groups.

The heuristic expert evaluation has shown that the results of the fifth configuration correspond most closely to reality. The scores of some languages, especially those in a more complicated political environment, do not yet adequately represent their language community's context. These results can be improved using the suggestions presented. The result of this initial approach provides a first starting point from which further development regarding aspects as clarity and reproducibility can be pursued.

Acknowledgments

The work presented in this article was co-financed by the European Union under grant agreement no. LC-01641480 – 101018166.

7 Bibliographical References

Aldabe, I., Rehm, G., Rigau, G., and Way, A. (2021). D3.1 Report on existing strategic documents and projects in LT/AI. https://european-language-equality.eu/wp-content/uploads/2021/12/ELE___Deliverable_D3_1__revised_.pdf.

Bali, K., Choudhury, M., Sitaram, S., and Seshadri, V. (2019). ELLORA: Enabling Low Resource Languages with Technology. In *Proceedings of the 1st International Conference on Language Technologies for All*, pages 160–163, Paris, France. European Language Resources Association.

Bargaoanu, A., Buturoiu, R., and Durach, F. (2019). The East-West Divide in the European Union: A Development Divide Reframed as a Political One. In Paul Dobrescu, editor, *Development in Turbulent Times: The Many Faces of Inequality Within Europe*, pages 105–118, Cham. Springer International Publishing.

Bielinska-Dusza, E. and Hamerska, M. (2021). Methodology for Calculating the European Innovation Scoreboard - Proposition for Modification. *Sustainability*, 13(4).

Blasi, D., Anastasopoulos, A., and Neubig, G. (2021). Systematic Inequalities in Language Technology Performance across the World's Languages. https://arxiv.org/abs/2110.06733.

Bromham, L., Dinnage, R., Skirgård, H., Ritchie, A., Cardillo, M., Meakins, F., Greenhill, S., and Hua, X. (2021). Global predictors of language endangerment and the future of linguistic diversity. *Nature Ecology & Evolution*, 6:163–173.

Burchardt, A., Egg, M., Eichler, K., Krenn, B., Kreutel, J., Leßmöllmann, A., Rehm, G., Stede, M., Uszkoreit, H., and Volk, M. (2012). *Die Deutsche Sprache im digitalen Zeitalter – The German Language in the Digital Age*. META-NET White Paper Series: Europe's Languages in the Digital Age. Springer, Heidelberg, New York, Dordrecht, London.

EU Publications Office. (2017a). EuroMatrix: Statistical and Hybrid Machine Translation Between All European Languages. https://cordis.europa.eu/project/id/034291. Last accessed: 07.02.2022.

EU Publications Office. (2017b). Internet Translators for all European Languages. https://cordis.europa.eu/project/id/250405. Last accessed: 07.02.2022.

European Parliament and Council of the European Union. (2019). Directive (EU) 2019/1024 of the European Parliament and of the Council of 20 June 2019 on open data and the re-use of public sector information. https://eur-lex.europa.eu/legal-content/EN/ALL/?uri=CELEX:32019L1024. Last accessed: 04.02.2022.

European Parliament. (2018). Language Equality in the Digital Age. European Parliament resolution of 11 September 2018 on Language Equality in the Digital Age (2018/2028(INI)). http://www.europarl.europa.eu/doceo/document/TA-8-2018-0332_EN.pdf. Last accessed: 02.02.2022.

European Union. (1992). European Charter for Regional or Minority Languages. *Council Of Europe European Treaty Series*, 148.

European Union. (2010). Charter of fundamental rights of the european union. *Official Journal of the European Union C83*, 53.

Faisal, F., Wang, Y., and Anastasopoulos, A. (2021). Dataset Geography: Mapping Language Data to Language Users. *Computing Research Repository (CoRR)*, abs/2112.03497. Last accessed: 10.02.2021.

Gaspari, F., Way, A., Dunne, J., Rehm, G., Piperidis, S., and Giagkou, M. (2021). D1.1 Digital Language Equality (preliminary definition). https://european-language-equality.eu/wp-content/uploads/2021/05/ELE_Deliverable_D1_1.pdf.

Gaspari, F., Gallagher, O., Rehm, G., Giagkou, M., Piperidis, S., Dunne, J., and Way, A. (2022). Introducing the Digital Language Equality Metric: Technological Factors. In Itziar Aldabe, et al., editors, *Proceedings of the Workshop Towards Digital Language Equality (TDLE 2022; co-located with LREC 2022)*, Marseille, France. Accepted for publication. 20 June 2022.

Georgsson, M., Weir, C. R., and Staggers, N. (2014). Revisiting Heuristic Evaluation Methods to Improve the Reliability of Findings. *Studies in health technology and informatics*, 205:930–934.

Hammarström, H., Forkel, R., Haspelmath, M., and Bank, S. (2021). *Glottolog 4.5*. Max Planck Institute for Evolutionary Anthropology, Leipzig. Last accessed: 09.02.2022.

Hinrichs, E. and Krauwer, S. (2014). The CLARIN Research Infrastructure: Resources and Tools for eHumanities Scholars. In *Proceedings of the Ninth International Conference on Language Resources and Evaluation (LREC-2014)*, pages 1525–1531, Reykjavik, Iceland. European Language Resources Association.

Joshi, P., Santy, S., Budhiraja, A., Bali, K., and Choudhury, M. (2020). The State and Fate of Linguistic Diversity and Inclusion in the NLP World. In *Proceedings of the 58th Annual Meeting of the Association for Computational Linguistics*, pages 6282–6293, Online. Association for Computational Linguistics.

Krauwer, S. (2003). The Basic Language Resource Kit (BLARK) as the First Milestone for the Language Resources Roadmap. In *Proceedings of SPECOM 2003*, Moscow, Russia. Moscow State Linguistic University.

Mager, M., Gutierrez-Vasques, X., Sierra, G., and Meza-Ruiz, I. (2018). Challenges of language technologies for the indigenous languages of the Americas. In *Proceedings of the 27th International Conference on Computational Linguistics*, pages 55–69, Santa Fe, New Mexico, USA. Association for Computational Linguistics.

Nielsen, J. and Molich, R., (1990). *Heuristic Evaluation of User Interfaces*, page 249–256. CHI '90. Association for Computing Machinery, New York, USA.

Rehm, G., Uszkoreit, H., Ananiadou, S., Bel, N., Bielevičienė, A., Borin, L., Branco, A., Budin, G., Calzolari, N., Daelemans, W., Garabík, R., Grobelnik, M., García-Mateo, C., Hajič, J., Hernáez, I., Judge, J., Koeva, S., Krek, S., Krstev, C., and Mc-Naught, J. (2014). The Strategic Impact of META-NET on the Regional, National and International Level. In *Language Resources and Evaluation*, volume 50.

Rehm, G., Berger, M., Elsholz, E., Hegele, S., Kintzel, F., Marheinecke, K., Piperidis, S., Deligiannis, M., Galanis, D., Gkirtzou, K., Labropoulou, P., Bontcheva, K., Jones, D., Roberts, I., Hajič, J., Hamrlová, J., Kačena, L., Choukri, K., Arranz, V., Vasiļjevs, A., Anvari, O., Lagzdiņš, A., Meļņika, J., Backfried, G., Dikici, E., Janosik, M., Prinz, K., Prinz, C., Stampler, S., Thomas-Aniola, D., Gómez-Pérez, J. M., Garcia Silva, A., Berrío, C., Germann, U., Renals, S., and Klejch, O. (2020a). European Language Grid: An Overview. In *Proceedings of the 12th Language Resources and Evaluation Conference*, pages 3366–3380, Marseille, France. European Language Resources Association.

Rehm, G., Marheinecke, K., Hegele, S., Piperidis, S., Bontcheva, K., Hajic, J., Choukri, K., Vasiļjevs, A., Backfried, G., Prinz, C., Pérez, J. M. G., Meertens, L., Lukowicz, P., van Genabith, J., Lösch, A., Slusallek, P., Irgens, M., Gatellier, P., Köhler, J., Bars, L. L., Anastasiou, D., Auksoriūtė, A., Bel, N., Branco, A., Budin, G., Daelemans, W., Smedt, K. D., Garabík, R., Gavriilidou, M., Gromann, D., Koeva, S., Krek, S., Krstev, C., Lindén, K., Magnini, B., Odijk, J., Ogrodniczuk, M., Rögnvaldsson, E., Rosner, M., Pedersen, B., Skadina, I., Tadić, M., Tufiș, D., Váradi, T., Vider, K., Way, A., and Yvon, F. (2020b). The European Language Technology Landscape in 2020: Language-Centric and Human-Centric AI for Cross-Cultural Communication in Multilingual Europe. In Nicoletta Calzolari, et al., editors, *Proceedings of the 12th Language Resources and Evaluation Conference (LREC 2020)*, pages 3315–3325, Marseille, France, 5. European Language Resources Association (ELRA).

Rehm, G. and Uszkoreit, H., editor. (2012). *META-NET White Paper Series: Europe's Languages in the Digital Age*, 32 volumes on 31 European languages, Heidelberg etc. Springer.

Rehm, G. and Way, A., editor. (2022). *European Language Equality: A Strategic Agenda for Digital Language Equality*. Cognitive Technologies. Springer. Forthcoming.

Rehm, G., editor. (2022). *European Language Grid: A Language Technology Platform for Multilingual Europe*. Cognitive Technologies. Springer. Forthcoming.

Romaine, S. (2017). Language Endangerment and Language Death. In *The Routledge Handbook of Ecolinguistics*, pages 40–55. Routledge.

Soria, C., Bel, N., Choukri, K., Mariani, J., Monachini, M., Odijk, J., Piperidis, S., Quochi, V., and Calzolari, N. (2012). The FLaReNet Strategic Language Resource Agenda. In *Proceedings of the Eighth International Conference on Language Resources and Evaluation (LREC'12)*, pages 1379–1386, Istanbul, Turkey. European Language Resources Association.

Stanford University. (2020). Global AI Vibrancy Tool. https://aiindex.stanford.edu/vibrancy/. Last accessed: 05.02.2022.

Stanford University. (2021). About: Developing a deeper understanding of a complex field. https://aiindex.stanford.edu/about/. Last accessed: 05.02.2022.

STOA. (2017). Language equality in the digital age – Towards a Human Language Project. http://www.europarl.europa.eu/stoa/. Last accessed: 13.01.2022.

Zhang, D., Mishra, S., Brynjolfsson, E., Etchemendy, J., Ganguli, D., Grosz, B., Lyons, T., Manyika, J., Niebles, J. C., Sellitto, M., Shoham, Y., Clark, J., and Perrault, R. (2021a). The AI Index 2021 Annual Report. https://aiindex.stanford.edu/report/. Last accessed: 05.02.2022.

Zhang, D., Mishra, S., Brynjolfsson, E., Etchemendy, J., Ganguli, D., Grosz, B., Lyons, T., Manyika, J., Niebles, J. C., Sellitto, M., Shoham, Y., Clark, J., and Perrault, R. (2021b). The AI Index 2021 Annual Report. https://arxiv.org/abs/2103.06312.

Appendix

Table 3: Initially proposed contextual factors (Gaspari et al., 2021)

Class	Factor	Indicator
Economy	Size of the economy	Annual GDP
		GDP per capita* **
	Size of the LT/NLP market	LT market in million Euro
	Size of the language service, translating or interpreting market	Number of organizations from the industry in the ELG catalogue* **
	Size of the IT/ICT sector	Perc. of the ICT sector in the GDP* **
		ICT service exports in Balance of Payment* **
	Investment instruments into AI/ LT	GDE on R&D in relevant areas*
	Regional/ national LT market	No indicator found
	Average socio-economic status	Annual net earnings, 1.0 FTE worker* **
		Life expectancy at age 60**
Education	Higher Education Institutions operating in the language	No indicator found
	Higher education in the language	No indicator found
	Academic positions in relevant areas	Head count of R&D personnel
	Academic programmes in relevant areas	No indicator found
	Literacy Level	Literacy rate*
	Students in language/LT/NLP curricula	Total no. of students in relevant areas* **
	Equity in education	Proportional tertiary educ. attainment* **
	Inclusion in education	Percentage of foreigners attaining tertiary education* **
Funding	Funding available for LT research projects	No. of projects funded in relevant areas*
		Score from the National funding programs
	Venture capital available	Venture capital amounts in Euro
	Public funding for interoperable platforms	Number of platforms**
Industry	Companies developing LTs	No. of enterprises in the field of I & C* **
	Start-ups per year	Percentage of "Enterprise births"**
	Start-ups in LT/ AI	Number of AI start ups* **
Law	Copyright legislation and regulations	No indicator found
	Legal status and legal protection	Scores out of the legal status* **
Media	Subtitled or dubbed visual media outcomes	Scores out of language transfer practices*
		Scores out of answers about broadcast practices
	Transcribed podcasts	Number of entries in the cba*
Online	Digital libraries	Percentage of contribution to Europeana
	Impact of language barriers on e-commerce	Percentage of population buying cross-border**
	Digital literacy	No indicator found
	Wikipedia pages	Number of articles in Wikipedia* **
	Websites exclusively in the language	No indicator found
	Websites in the language (not exclusively)	Perc. of websites in the languages* **
	Web pages	No indicator
	Ranking of websites delivering content	12 selected websites supporting the languages
	Labels and lemmas in knowledge bases	Number of lexemes in Wikipedia* **
	Language support gaps	Language matrix of supported features*
	Impact on E-commerce websites	T-Index*

Continued on next page

Table 3 – *Continued from previous page*

Class	Factor	Indicator
Policy	Presence of strategic plans, agendas, etc.	Scores out of a list of the published national AI strategies Scores from questionnaire about strategies
	Promotion of the LR ecosystem	No indicator found
	Consideration of bodies for the LR citation	No indicator found
	Promotion of cooperation	No indicator found
	Public and community support for resource production best practices	No indicator found
	Policies regarding BLARKs	No indicator found
	Political activity	Scores out of the list of documents
Public administration	Languages of public institutions	No. of constitutions written in the language
	Available public services in the language	Percentage of a maximum score about digital public services** Score for digital public services**
Research & Development & Innovation	Innovation capacity	Innovation Index* **
	Research groups in LT	Number of research organizations
	Research groups/ companies predominantly working on the respective language	No indicator found
	Research staff involved in LT	No indicator found
	Suitably qualified Research staff in LT	No indicator found
	Capacity for talent retention in LT	No indicator found
	State of play of NLP/AI	No indicator found
	Scientists working in LT/ on the language	Number of researchers in relevant areas*
	Researchers whose work benefits from LRs and LTs	No indicator found
	Overall research support staff	Head count of research support staff* **
	Scientific associations or general scientific and technology ecosystem	No indicator found
	Papers about LT and or the language	Number of papers about LT** Number of papers about the language* **
Society	Importance of the language	No indicator found
	Fully proficient (literate) speakers	Number of L1 speakers*
	Digital Skills	Perc. of individuals with basic digital skills* **
	Size of language community	Total number of speakers* **
	Population not speaking the official language(s)	No indicator found
	Official or recognized languages	Total no. of languages with official status* Number of bordering languages
	Community languages	Number of community languages*
	Time resources of the language community	No indicator found
	Society stakeholders for the language	No indicator found
	Speakers' attitudes towards the language	Total number of participants wanting to acquire the language
	Involvement of indigenous peoples	No indicator found
	Sensitivity to barriers	No indicator found
	Usage of Social Media or networks	Total number of social media users* ** Percentage of social media users* **
Technology	Open-source technologies of LTs	No indicator found
	Access to computer, smartphone etc.	Perc. of households with a computer* **
	Digital connectivity and Internet access	Perc. of households with broadband* **

*Indicator marked * is automatically updateable – Indicator marked ** provides data with good quality*

Table 4: Conversion from plain text to scores

Factor	Merging of scores	Conversion from Text to Scores
Public funding available for LTs	Adding up of the scores for each country	1 for regional funding 1 for national funding 1 for intranational funding 1 each for ESIF, EUREKA, EUROSTAT
Legal status and legal protection	Adding up of the scores per language	10 for statutory national language 10 for de facto national working language 2 for statutory provincial language 2 for statutory provincial working language 1 for recognized language
Publicly available media outcomes	Sum of two scores: one for language transfer practices for films screened, one for tv broadcasts	2 for dub 1.5 for voice over 1.5 for sub and dub 1 for sub
	Sum of the scores + division through number of answers	Broadcast in original language: 5 for mostly/ always, 2.5 for sometimes ... with dubbing: 4 for mostly/ always, 2 for sometimes ... in original language with voice-over: 3 for mostly/ always, 1.5 for sometimes ... with subtitles: 1 for mostly/ always, 0.5 for sometimes Dual-channel audio: 2 for mostly/ always, 1 for somet.
Presence of local, regional or national strategic plans	One of the score per country	1 for no plan/ strategy 2 for a plan without mentioning LT 3 for a plan mentioning LT 4 for a plan mentioning LT, minority, regional languages
Political activity	Adding up of the scores per country	1 score for each document (mentioning LT) 2 for each document exclusively about LT 1 for a document covering a specific language 2 for each document published 2020/2021 1 for each document published 2019/2018

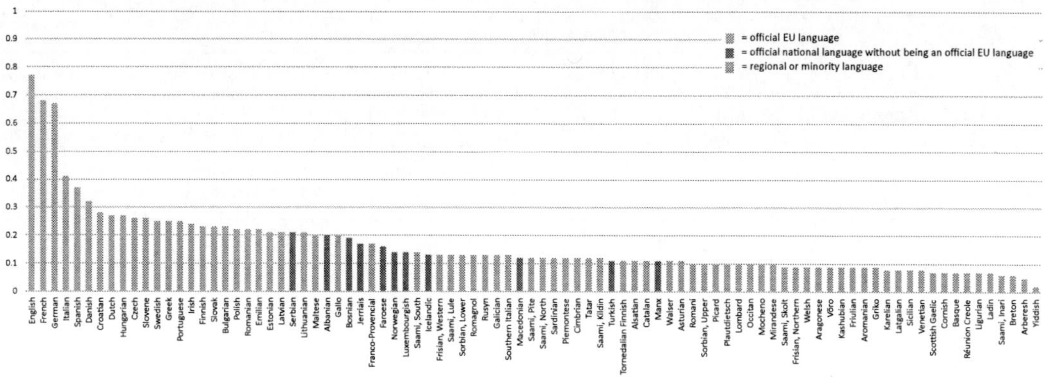

Results of Configuration 1 (46 factors with available data)

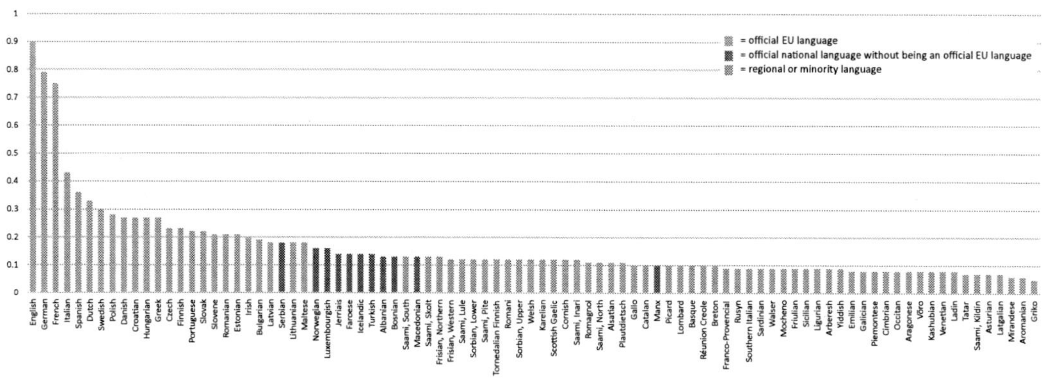

Results of Configuration 2 (34 factors that can be updated automatically)

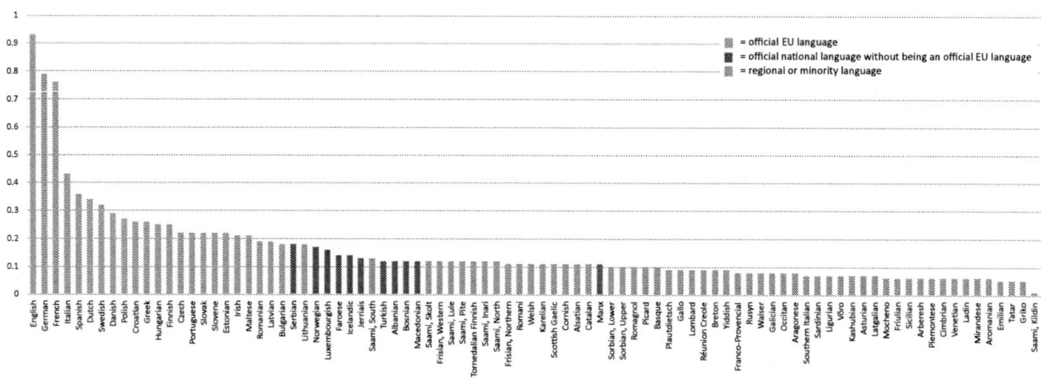

Results of Configuration 3 (26 factors with good data quality)

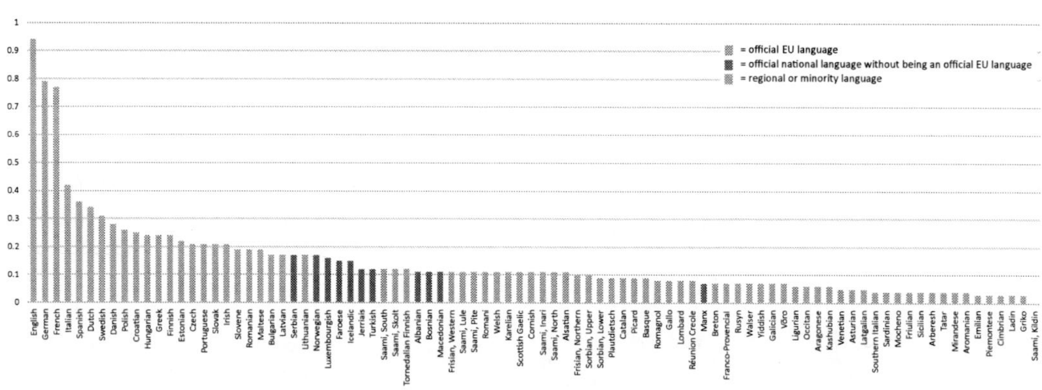

Results of Configuration 4 (21 factors that can be updated automatically and that have good data quality)

Figure 2: Results of Configurations 1 to 4

Proceedings of the TDLE Workshop @LREC2022, pages 27–35
Marseille, 20 June 2022

Collaborative Metadata Aggregation and Curation in Support of Digital Language Equality Monitoring

Maria Giagkou, Penny Labropoulou, Stelios Piperidis, Miltos Deligiannis, Athanasia Kolovou, Leon Voukoutis
Institute for Language and Speech Processing, Athena Research Centre
{mgiagkou, penny, spip, mdel, akolovou, leon.voukoutis}@athenarc.gr

Abstract

The European Language Equality (ELE) project develops a strategic research, innovation and implementation agenda (SRIA) and a roadmap for achieving full digital language equality in Europe by 2030. Key component of the SRIA development is an accurate estimation of the current standing of languages with respect to their technological readiness. In this paper we present the empirical basis on which such estimation is grounded, its starting point and in particular the automatic and collaborative methods used for extending it. We focus on the collaborative expert activities, the challenges posed, and the solutions adopted. We also briefly present the dashboard application developed for querying and visualising the empirical data as well as monitoring and comparing the evolution of technological support within and across languages.

Keywords: language resources, language technologies, metadata aggregation, digital language equality

1. Introduction

With a large and all-encompassing consortium consisting of 52 partners covering all European countries, research and industry and all major pan-European initiatives, the European Language Equality (ELE)[1] project develops a strategic research, innovation and implementation agenda (SRIA) as well as a roadmap for achieving full digital language equality in Europe by 2030. Key component of the SRIA development process is an as accurate as possible estimation of the current standing of languages spoken in Europe with respect to their technological readiness. In turn, such estimation presupposes the existence of the necessary data, resources and services that underlie and reflect onto technological readiness.

The META-NET White Papers series (Rehm and Uszkoreit, 2012) reported, back in 2012, that more than 21 European languages were in danger of digital extinction. Despite the vast improvements in language technology (LT) performance in the last couple of years, technology support for Europe's languages is still characterised by a stark imbalance. While many resources and technologies exist for English and some of the most widely spoken European languages, the majority of other languages still suffer from lack of technology support, as attested in the Language Reports series initiated by the ELE[2] (Giagkou et al., 2022). Digital Language Equality (DLE), as conceived in the ELE project, is defined as "the state of affairs in which all languages have the technological support and situational context necessary for them to continue to exist and to prosper as living languages in the digital age" (Gaspari et al., 2021). The Digital Language Equality (DLE) Metric (Gaspari et al., 2021, Gaspari et al., 2022) is a measure that reflects the digital readiness of a language and its contribution to the state of technology-enabled multilingualism, tracking its progress towards the goal of DLE. The DLE Metric is computed for each language on the basis of various factors, grouped into technological support (technological factors, e.g., count of the available language resources, tools and technologies) and a range of situational context factors (e.g., societal, economic, educational, industrial factors)[3].

In close collaboration with its sister project, the European Language Grid (ELG)[4] (Rehm et al., 2020; Rehm et al., 2021), ELE makes use of the ELG platform functionalities and catalogue contents as the empirical base for calculating the technological factors of the DLE metric. This decision is based on the fact that the ELG catalogue is Europe's most comprehensive registry of language resources and tools/services. Despite its comprehensiveness, the ELG catalogue is not exhaustive; language resources are produced at a much higher rate than ever before due to the dominant data driven methods in language technology research and development. In addition, a number of initiatives in Europe, domain specific and general, are engaged in data and service registration activities. Therefore, the decision has been made that the ELG platform and its catalogue are further enriched by two separate procedures: (a) harvesting existing catalogues of major infrastructures and initiatives in Europe (e.g., CLARIN, ELRC, Zenodo), and (b) by an unprecedented collaborative metadata collection procedure undertaken by language experts covering over 70 languages, i.e., all the EU official languages as well as a great number of Europe's regional and minority languages and dialects[5].

All metadata resulting from these enrichment activities are not only available through the ELG catalogue, but they are also queryable through a dashboard. The ELE dashboard allows to interactively visualise the indicators of the level of LT support for the languages covered by the project, providing a detailed, empirical and dynamic map of technology support for European languages and dialects.

This paper discusses the processes used for extending the coverage of the ELG catalogue, the challenges posed, and the solutions adopted. Section 2 briefly presents the contents of the ELG catalogue and the automatic processes

[1] https://european-language-equality.eu/

[2] The research partners have prepared updates of the META-NET White Papers (Rehm and Uszkoreit, 2012) available at https://european-language-equality.eu/deliverables/ including the results of the survey.

[3] For the full list of the factors, see Gaspari et al. (2022).

[4] https://www.european-language-grid.eu/

[5] https://european-language-equality.eu/languages/

that were put in place in order to enrich the catalogue's coverage mainly through harvesting protocols and API-based access to catalogues of major European infrastructures, platforms, and initiatives. Section 3 elaborates on the collaborative metadata collection process initiated by ELE and Section 4 briefly sketches a relaxed version of the ELG metadata schema[6] (Labropoulou et al. 2020) to accommodate input from lighter schemata. In Section 5, we briefly present the ELE dashboard, and conclude with some general observations and plans for the future.

2. ELG catalogue and automatic enrichment procedures

The European Language Grid tries to tackle the observed fragmentation in the European Language Technology landscape (Soria et al. 2012) by bringing together Language Resources and Technologies (LRTs) and to support and boost the LT sector and LT activities in Europe through multiple multilevel services. ELG already provides a scalable cloud-based platform[7] through which developers and providers of LRTs can not only deposit and upload them into the ELG, but also deploy them through the grid platform. ELG offers access already to thousands of commercial and non-commercial LTs and ancillary Language Resources (LRs) for all European languages and more; these include processing and generation services, tools, applications for written and spoken language, as well as corpora, different types of lexical resources, language models and computational grammars, etc.

For the further population of the catalogue of its platform, ELG has built bridges to existing initiatives and reaches agreements for harvesting and importing information (aka metadata) and resources from other infrastructures, platforms and repositories under mutually agreed conditions and attribution of the source.

Currently, ELG has implemented a client compliant with the Open Archives Initiative Protocol for Metadata Harvesting[8] (OAI-PMH) (Lagoze et al. 2012) that supports harvesting from other repositories which expose their metadata via an ELG-compatible OAI-PMH endpoint.

OAI-PMH is used for harvesting LINDAT/CLARIAH-CZ[9], i.e., the Czech CLARIN national node, as well as the Polish (CLARIN-PL[10]) and Slovene (CLARIN-SI[11]) CLARIN nodes, given that they use the same repository software as LINDAT. Such harvesting procedure benefits from the fact that the ELG metadata model (Labropoulou et al., 2020) builds on the META-SHARE metadata model (Gavrilidou et al., 2012), while the LINDAT DSpace software supports the export of metadata in the META-SHARE minimal schema.

The same harvesting approach is followed for the harvesting of metadata records from the ELRC-SHARE repository[12], which is used for the storage of and access to language resources collected through the European Language Resource Coordination[13] initiative (Lösch et al., 2018) and considered useful for feeding the CEF Automated Translation (CEF.AT) platform[14]. The ELRC-SHARE repository (Piperidis et al., 2018) uses a metadata schema based on the META-SHARE schema tuned to text resources for Machine Translation purposes.

A different procedure (Figure 1) has been implemented for Hugging Face[15] (Wolf et al., 2019), which includes a large collection of Machine Learning (ML) models and datasets that can be used for training models, with a focus on transformers. Hugging Face exposes two distinct APIs with JSON files for datasets and models respectively, including a subset of the metadata elements displayed on their catalogue. However, not all records have values for all of the elements. Since importing into ELG presupposes that at least the mandatory elements of the minimal version are filled in, the conversion and import of records from Hugging Face into ELG has so far been restricted to datasets with at least the description, language and licence elements filled in, as these are deemed the minimum threshold for findability and usability purposes in ELG. A conversion process has been set up based on the mapping of the elements and controlled vocabularies values. Further enrichment of the resulting records has been performed for specific elements, notably the licencing information, while, where required, default values have been used for mandatory elements whose values could not be inferred from the original metadata records (e.g., all datasets have been assigned the "text" value for "media type"). Records for which the above processes did not render the mandatory elements were discarded.

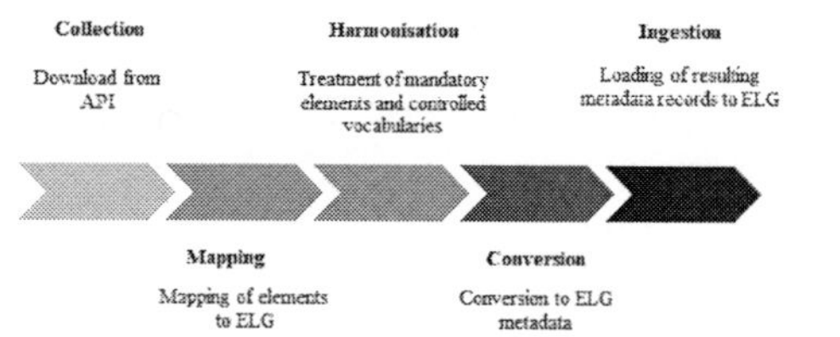

Figure 1: Workflow for the import of Hugging Face metadata records into ELG

General repositories like Zenodo[16] pose different challenges, the main one being as precise as possible filtering of the candidate records. Zenodo exposes metadata records in two channels: through a REST API[17], which outputs records as JSON files, and an OAI-PMH API[18] in a set of standard metadata formats, namely DC[19] (International Organization for Standardization 2017), DataCite[20] (DataCite Metadata Working Group 2021),

[6] https://gitlab.com/european-language-grid/platform/ELG-SHARE-schema
[7] https://live.european-language-grid.eu/
[8] https://www.openarchives.org/pmh/
[9] https://lindat.mff.cuni.cz/
[10] https://clarin-pl.eu/dspace/
[11] https://www.clarin.si/repository/xmlui/?locale-attribute=en
[12] https://www.elrc-share.eu/
[13] https://lr-coordination.eu/
[14] https://language-tools.ec.europa.eu/
[15] https://huggingface.co/
[16] https://zenodo.org/
[17] https://developers.zenodo.org/#rest-api
[18] https://developers.zenodo.org/#oai-pmh
[19] https://www.dublincore.org/specifications/dublin-core/dcmi-terms/
[20] https://schema.datacite.org/

MARC21[21] (Library of Congress 1999) and DCAT[22] (Albertoni et al. 2020). With regard to import, the preferred solution is the OAI-PMH protocol, which is rate limited, hence not appropriate for big amounts of metadata records. We have, therefore, resorted to a combined solution: we have downloaded the automatically generated full dump of 2,060,674 metadata records included in Zenodo until 31/08/2021. For records added to Zenodo after this date, we are incrementally harvesting from the OAI-PMH endpoint, adding 147,621 records during a four-month period. From the resulting 2,208,295 metadata records available until 31/12/2021, 592,509 entries of type "dataset" and "software" were filtered; we are experimenting with high-precision filtering methods on these to identify records of interest for LT purposes. The conversion of the metadata records is based on the DCAT metadata schema, the richest among the ones exposed by Zenodo, while certain relaxations of the ELG schema proved necessary to take into account the DCAT features (see Section 4). Figure 2 depicts the workflow for metadata records downloaded from the OAI-PMH server.

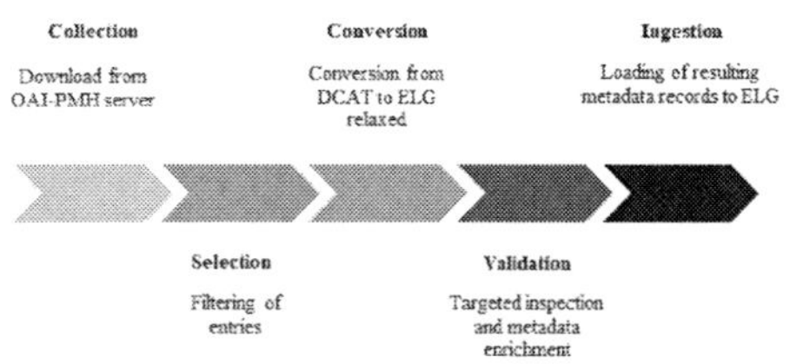

Figure 2: Workflow for the import of the Zenodo metadata records into ELG

At the time of writing, the ELG catalogue includes 977 metadata records harvested from the CLARIN nodes, and 1,299 records from ELRC-SHARE. In addition, 385 records for datasets have been imported from Hugging Face, while the conversion for models is ongoing, as is the import from Zenodo.

3. Collaborative ELE metadata collection

With the ELG Catalogue as basis and point of departure, ELE initiated a large-scale metadata collection activity in order to create an as representative as possible base on which the technological readiness of languages spoken in Europe would be estimated. At least 40 different organisations[23], ELE consortium members and other collaborators of the partners' networks, acted as language expert informants for one of the official, co-official, regional, minority and community European languages. They investigated, discovered, and appropriately documented LRTs that contribute to a language's level of technological support. These include LT tools and services, as well as language resources that can be used for the development of LT, i.e., corpora and datasets, language descriptions (language models and computational grammars), and lexical/conceptual resources. Given the availability of the respective information, the language informants additionally recorded the research or industrial providers of LRTs and the project(s) in the framework of which the LRTs have been developed.

3.1 ELE metadata collection instruments

The ELE partners were asked to only document resources that were not already included in the ELG catalogue and were thus provided with a list of its contents at the time of conducting the metadata collection.

They were given the option to describe the resources they discovered using the metadata editor which is available in the ELG platform, and/or an online form[24], and/or a spreadsheet which was automatically populated by the responses to the online form and accessible for direct manual editing and bulk import of records.

The online form (and linked spreadsheet) was appropriately configured to render a very simplified version of the ELG metadata schema. By adhering to and utilising the ELG schema, interoperability with the ELG platform was guaranteed, thus allowing for the aggregation and ingestion of the LRTs documented by the ELE partners into ELG in an as automated as possible manner. On the other hand, having set as a priority the documentation of as many LRTs as possible over a detailed documentation for each of them, and in order to respond to the variety of sources from which the ELE informants would discover relevant information, only a subset of the ELG metadata categories have been included in the ELE online form. These were carefully selected to elicit sufficient information for the ELE purposes.

The online form contained the following metadata categories (elements marked with an asterisk were mandatory):

- identification: *resource type**, *resource name**, *resource short name*, *landing page**, *description**, *publication year*, *resource provider (organisation name)*
- contact data: *name & homepage of source*, *contact email*
- classification: *keyword*, *domain*
- funding information: *funding project* & *funding type*
- usage information: *licence*, *access rights*
- technical information for data resources: *subclass**, *language** and, where applicable, *geographical variety*, *multilinguality type*, *media type**, *size*; in addition, for annotated corpora, *annotation type*, and, for lexical/conceptual resources, *encoding level*
- technical information for tools/services: *function**, *Technological Readiness Level (TRL)*, whether they are *language independent**, and if not, the *language* and, where applicable, *geographical variety* of the input resource, *media type* of the input resource, and, optionally, *language*, *geographical variety* and *media type* of the output resource.

Recommended controlled vocabularies, in the form of lists of values from which users could select a value, were used where possible (e.g., for language), yet informants could also add free text values. Depending on the element, adding multiple values was possible (e.g., for domains,

[21] https://www.loc.gov/marc/bibliographic/
[22] https://www.w3.org/TR/vocab-dcat-2/
[23] https://european-language-equality.eu/languages/
[24] The online form template is available at https://forms.gle/WjJZ1CZqXDPQjPHA8

languages, keywords, etc.) Mandatory elements were marked as such with validation imposed.

3.2 Curation process

This systematic collection resulted **in 6,790 new metadata records created by the ELE language experts**. Before being imported to the ELG database, these records were curated (Figure 3). The curation process concerned (semi-) automatic and manual processing of the records with the aim to ensure that they adhere to the "relaxed" version of the ELG metadata schema (Section 4) and that they can be imported in the catalogue, as well as to harmonise values and thus enhance their discoverability and contribute to more reliable statistics.

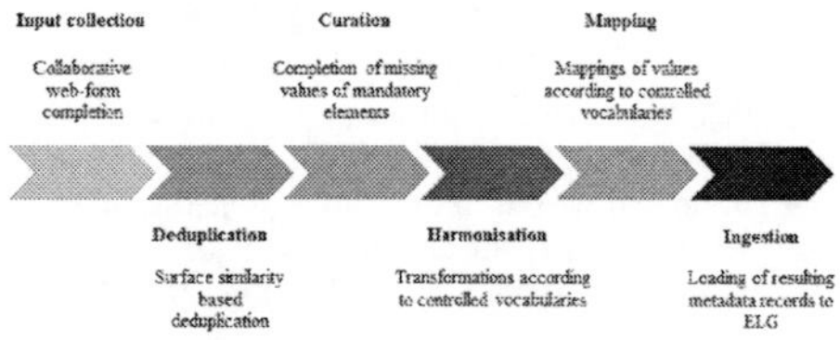

Figure 3: Workflow for the import of the ELE survey results into ELG

3.2.1 Deduplication

Duplicate records were identified first by checking the resource name, and then by inspecting those that had the same resource short name and landing page. We thus identified duplicates that had different names (e.g. "Corpus Web Salud Español" - "Spanish Biomedical Crawled Corpus", "Comprehensive Estonian-French Dictionary" - "Grand dictionnaire estonien-français"). Some records were identified as duplicates of existing ELG records while others were duplicates of other ELE informants' contributions. When the duplicate records contained different or contradicting values, e.g., different functions, licences, etc. the source was consulted, and the record was manually corrected.

3.2.2 Completion of mandatory metadata

The ELG metadata schema includes a set of mandatory elements deemed important for the documentation of LRTs, e.g., resource name, description, language and media type. Missing values in mandatory metadata result in invalid records and failure of import to the database. To minimise loss of data due to missing mandatory values, we resorted to a combination of solutions:

- We used heuristics to add the missing values, where possible. For instance, using the size unit values, keywords and/or hints in the description or resource name we automatically inferred and assigned the media type value; e.g., "text" was selected for records with size unit values such as articles, translation units, texts, etc., or containing the terms "web corpus", "Wikipedia", etc. in the description or in the resource name.
- If no value could be automatically assigned, we consulted the source and manually filled in the missing values, where possible.
- For remaining records, when the data type of the element permitted this, we used the value "unspecified".

3.2.3 Harmonisation and mapping of metadata values

The ELG schema adopts controlled vocabularies for the value space of specific metadata elements (e.g., media type, language, service function, annotation type, size unit, etc.). For some of them (e.g., service function), free text values added by users are also allowed.

During the curation, where possible and appropriate, the free text values added by ELE informants were semi-automatically mapped to values of the controlled vocabularies or aggregated under the same value. For instance, values such as "speech synthesis", "speech synthesizer", "text to speech", "TtS" for the service function element were all mapped to "Speech synthesis". For certain elements (e.g., for "domain"), broader terms were also added, to improve findability. For instance, records with the domain values "travel", "transport" "geography", "hotel" were assigned also the value "Geography, Travel & Tourism".

In addition, in the case of closed controlled vocabularies, i.e., vocabularies that do not allow the use of free text values, unmappable values left as is would result in invalid metadata records. Therefore, for specific elements deemed important for the adequate representation of resources, we manually inspected the description of the records and/or source in order to select the appropriate value. This is the case, for instance, of the element "subclass" used to distinguish models from computational grammars, as well as of "language", which is discussed in Section 3.2.4.

Moreover, in a first attempt to narrow down the wide range of size units used, for text corpora that specified size in sentences, an additional size in words was computed based on the calculation of average sentence length in words, per language, in the Universal Dependency Treebank.

Finally, despite the harmonization of service function values, the list was deemed too long for eliciting meaningful statistical observations. For ELE purposes, a set of six higher-order concepts were put forward: "Text Processing", "Speech Processing", "Translation Technologies", "Image/Video Processing", "Human Computer Interaction", "Natural Language Generation", "Information Extraction and Information Retrieval", "Support operation" and "Other". Given the fact that the values of the metadata element "service function" are from the OMTD-SHARE ontology[25] (Labropoulou et al., 2018), and most specifically the "Function" class, the grouping of the values has been made at the ontology side, and thus used for all tools and services included in the ELG catalogue. Some of the group values were already included in the ontology, but the classification of the functions could not serve ELE purposes as is. We thus decided to represent the groups as SKOS Collections and not interfere with the existing hierarchy.

3.2.4 Treatment of language values

Language occupies a central place among the documentation elements for language resources and tools. Its standardisation is therefore important while its value space must cater for the representation of language

[25] http://w3id.org/meta-share/omtd-share/

varieties, regional variants, idiolects, time delimited language forms, etc. The ELG schema has adopted the RFC recommendation[26] (Phillips and Davis, 2009), which combines the ISO 639 vocabulary[27] (International Organization for Standardization, 2007) with additional subtags for region, script and variants. Yet there are still language varieties not covered by even the ISO 639-3 part[28] (the most extensive part of the ISO 639 standard). For this reason, we use two additional elements, namely the element "glottolog code" which takes values from the Glottolog vocabulary[29] (Hammarström et al., 2021) and the "language variety" element, which takes free text values. These elements are used alongside the language subtag in the following way:

- When there's an equivalence link between the ISO value and the Glottolog code, both are added at the respective elements and the language name displayed on the ELG catalogue is that of the official name from the ISO list; this has the benefit that we can exploit alternative names from the linked data contained in Glottolog for the enhancement of search functionalities.
- If a language variety (e.g., "Abenaki") is not included in the ISO list, the value "mis" (uncoded languages) is used for the ISO value element, the Glottolog code is added and the language name displayed on the ELG catalogue is derived from Glottolog, thus serving as an additional standardization measure.
- If a language variety is not included in either of the two (e.g., "Valbonnais dialect"), the respective language name is added to the "language variety" element.

For the ELE web form, we decided to ask informants to document only the language(s) and optionally the country/region subtags of the LRTs, where appropriate and necessary. For instance, if they needed to document a resource containing Austrian German, they could indicate "German" as the language value and "Austria" as the geographical variety value. For the "language" element we added as valid values the set of names of the European languages targeted by the project, and also allowed for user added values, so that they could add languages from other countries and language varieties.

The output records included many free text values, even for cases included in the pre-filled values (e.g., alternative values such as "Greek", "Modern Greek", "el", "ell", values from different parts of the ISO 639 vocabulary, typos, etc.). Unique language values were extracted from the list and mapped to the controlled vocabularies according to the policy described above. To do so, we went through a series of repeated rounds of automatic checks, based on exact and similar match to the language identifiers and names from the ISO 639 and Glottolog vocabularies, and manual inspection and corrections[30].

The "language geographical variety" values were also harmonized and mapped to the ISO 3166 country codes[31] when possible. For regions without an ISO code (e.g., "Lower Saxony"), a value was filled in at the "language variety" element (e.g., "Variety in Lower Saxony").

3.2.5 Treatment of licensing information

Licensing information is critical for the (re-)usability of any resource and thus required in the ELG schema. For the ELE survey, anticipating that the licence value might be difficult to fill in, the web form included the "licence" element with a list of the most popular standard licences and an option for adding free text, as well as the "access rights" element with a choice between three values, namely "Licensed without a fee for all uses", "Licensed without a fee for specific uses" and "Licensed with a fee". Informants were asked to fill in at least the "access rights", which is required in the "relaxed" version of the schema (see Section 4); for standard licences, the mapping to the "access rights" would be provided by the ELG/ELE core team.

However, both elements were filled in with diverging values that needed to be harmonised and mapped in the follow up curation process. Specifically:

- Use of alternative values for the same licence (e.g., "CC-BY-4.0", "Creative commons attribution 4", etc.)
- Reference to a licence with multiple versions, without any indication of the specific version (e.g., "Creative commons attribution").
- Reference to a non-standard licence by name and no further information on the licensing terms or a hyperlink to the licence text
- Use of a free text value for licence and/or access rights besides the ELE recommended ones, such as "free for academic use", "available for research", "Copyright 2012", "not currently accessible to the public", etc.
- Total absence of a value for both elements.

Overall more than 300 values in these two elements could not be matched to known licences. Through semi-automatic and manual checks, often through searches for the specific licences, we have curated both elements, keeping the "licence" element as originally conceived in ELG (i.e., with a name and URL) and extending the notion of "access rights" to allow for any free text value. Thus, "licence" was used only when a URL with the licensing terms was found and alternative names were all mapped to a single value; if available, the name as it appears in the SPDX list of licences[32] was selected. Licences with an unspecified version were harmonized (e.g., "Creative Commons Attribution") and added as "access rights" values. Records with no licence and no access rights were added with the value "unspecified" for the access rights.

An additional element, namely "condition of use", is used for the representation of licensing information. This element takes values from a subset of popular conditions of use associated with licences (e.g., no derivatives, non-commercial use, etc.) and is deemed important for findability purposes. It was additionally deemed necessary for the calculation of the technological part of the DLE

[26] https://datatracker.ietf.org/doc/html/rfc5646

[27] https://www.iso.org/iso-639-language-codes.html

[28] https://iso639-3.sil.org/

[29] https://glottolog.org/

[30] From the initial 1,147 unique language values contained in the spreadsheet, only 937 were matched with languages in the ISO 639 set at the first step. For all remaining values, a semi-automatic curation was required, resulting in 1,263 unique values.

[31] https://www.iso.org/iso-3166-country-codes.html

[32] https://spdx.org/licenses/

metric, as it provided a higher-level representation and approximation of the "openness" scale of language resources. The appropriate "conditions of use" values are assigned to standard licences by the ELG legal team, or, in the case of non-standard licences, by the metadata creators when they describe a resource. The "access rights" values added through the ELE metadata collection have also been mapped to the same values supporting queries about resource accessibility in the DLE dashboard (Section 5).

3.3 Metadata conversion and ingestion

During metadata curation and processing, approximately 400 records of the initial 6,790 records have been discarded, mainly because of duplicates or incomplete mandatory metadata that could not be recovered.
The remaining records were automatically converted into ELG-compliant metadata records. As a result, **6,362 records** have been imported into ELG, consisting of 2,215 metadata records describing LT tools/services and 4,147 records describing data resources, i.e., corpora, lexical/conceptual resources and language descriptions (grammars or language models). They cover all the languages addressed by the ELE language reports series (Giagkou et al., 2022), i.e., the 24 official EU languages plus some other (co)official languages at the national or regional level (Norwegian, Icelandic, Serbian, Bosnian, Basque, Catalan and Galician), as well as the additional languages and dialects targeted by the ELE project.
All the metadata records are marked in the ELG catalogue as "for information", indicating that they include only a limited set of metadata elements, and they can be "claimed" for further enrichment by their owners, following the respective ELG policies and operations. Dissemination activities have been undertaken to inform persons designated as contact points for these resources as well as the broader community members about the ELE metadata collection results and their import into ELG.

3.4 Organisations and projects

Although the ELE survey focused on LRTs, the information collected was also used for the enrichment of the ELG inventory of organizations and projects, which are then automatically linked with their related LRTs in the ELG Catalogue.
More specifically, the element "resource provider" contains companies, academic institutions, public institutions, etc. that are active in the LT domain. After a round of cleanup (e.g., person and project names were included among the values) and harmonization (e.g., for alternative names and typos), these were imported and they are published in the catalogue.
A similar process of curation is ongoing for the publication of the funding projects. This process seeks to add missing mandatory values and assign the mixture of values that were filled in for "project name" to the appropriate metadata elements; indicatively, this was filled in with project names in various languages, identifiers, grant award numbers, funder names, funding programmes, etc.

4. Metadata schema adaptations

Achieving metadata interoperability across repositories is a challenging task due to the diversity and granularity of schemas used by different communities, intended purposes, types of resources described, etc. and various methods are utilized to address it (Alemu et al. 2012, Chan & Zeng 2006, Broeder et al. 2019, McCrae et al. 2015, Zeng & Chan 2006). The approach presented in this paper is based on the mapping of the source schemas into the target (ELG) schema, as well as on the enrichment of the source records with information required when this is possible without misconceptions and inconsistencies. Yet, this does not suffice for automatically aggregating records from the sources presented above.
More specifically, to be imported into the ELG platform, metadata records must comply with the minimal version of the ELG schema, i.e., the values must respect the designated data type of the elements and at least some mandatory metadata elements must be filled in. However, for metadata records automatically imported from other catalogues and repositories, as well as in sizable collaborative initiatives, such as the metadata collection undertaken by the ELE experts, the demand for filling in even the minimal version was considered challenging. The modifications required to accommodate such a collaborative population scenario resulted in the "relaxed" version, which can only be used in such cases.
The "relaxed" version of the ELG metadata schema aims to accommodate "mismatches" between the ELG schema and schemas with lighter information requirements. The main features characterising this version are the introduction of alternative elements for mandatory metadata elements that may be missing from the source records or elements that have different data types.
The first case refers to two elements that are deemed important for ELG purposes: "media type" and "licence".

- The "media type part" element is crucial for ELG purposes, as it is used for attaching important metadata properties, such as language, format, size, etc. Therefore, even in cases where these elements are included in the source records, they cannot be imported into ELG if the "media type part" value is missing. For these cases, the value "unspecified media part" can be used.
- Licence is crucial for re-usability purposes; for a licence, both a name and a URL hyperlink to the legal document with the terms and conditions are required. However, in many cases, such as legacy resources, or records in catalogues allowing free text as licence value, these two elements cannot be determined. Therefore, the "access rights" element that takes a free text value may be filled in as an alternative to "licence", specifying the rights of access and use at a higher level of abstraction.

The second case refers to metadata properties, such as size, which in the ELG schema are represented as a combination of two elements – "amount" and "sizeUnit"– while in other schemas and catalogues a single free text element is used. In this case, a new element that takes free text as a value (e.g., "sizeText") has been added in the schema as an alternative to the combination.

5. ELE dashboard

To provide a mechanism for exposing and monitoring the technological (TFs) and contextual factors (CFs) that contribute to the DLE metric (Gaspari et al., 2022), we designed and implemented an interactive dashboard as part of the ELG platform. The dashboard exposes the TFs (based on the contents of the ELG catalogue) and the CFs as interactive visuals dynamically created by user queries. With regard to the TFs, as the ELG catalogue organically grows over time, the resulting DLE Metric scores will be updated for all European languages, thereby providing an up-to-date and consistent measurement of the level of LT support and provision that each of them enjoys, also showing where the status is less than ideal or not at the expected level. Similarly, the situational indicators that are reflected by the CFs will be updated for the relevant languages on up-to-date data, as it becomes available from the selected sources.

The user interface of the ELE dashboard, which can be accessed through the ELG platform[33], consists of three entry points (sections). The first section displays the bar graphs of the DLE metrics for CFs and TFs for the languages selected by the user (see for instance Figure 4 in the Appendix). In the other two sections users can dive into a more detailed comparison of a subset of the TFs across languages and within a language respectively. The comparison can be made on datasets vs. software resources and, by selecting one of the two, for a number of features characteristic of the corresponding resource class. For datasets, these are the resource subclass, the linguality type, the media type and the access rights. For software, the available query criteria are: service function groups, input and output media types and access rights.

Architecturally, the ELE dashboard consists of two layers. The ELG database provides the source data to be exposed, in particular the source data for the technological factors that contribute to DLE. The ELG database contents are indexed and saved in appropriate JSON structures. Each user query retrieves the respective results from JSON and exposes them to the front end. The calculated scores pre language for the contextual part of the DLE metric are stored in a separate file and exposed to the respective tab of the dashboard front end.

All results are visualised as graphs. For the front end implementation, the react-chartjs-2[34] library for charts and the chartjs-plugin-zoom[35] library for additional features like pan and zoom options on a chart have been selected.

6. Conclusions and future plans

In this paper we have presented the methods used to construct the empirical basis on which the technological readiness of languages spoken in Europe can be estimated. With the catalogue of the ELG Platform as point of departure, we have presented the automatic and collaborative language expert-based enrichment activities, so that the empirical basis is as representative as possible. We have also discussed the challenges emerging when such large-scale metadata aggregation activities are undertaken as well as the techniques used to mitigate them. While it is becoming clear that the language resources and technologies community is gradually converging to common metadata-based documentation practices, such that this work has been possible in the end, technical and semantic interoperability issues still remain and further standardisation will only make such aggregation activities more robust, efficient and cost-effective. The automatic enrichment procedures of the ELG catalogue put in place will continue at regular intervals, ensuring that the empirical basis for monitoring the level of digital readiness of languages is expanding in proportion to community activities and achievements. In parallel, the technical means made available through the ELG Platform will help keeping the empirical basis as up to date as possible through hopefully easy to use data and metadata registration functionalities.

We have also presented the ongoing work on the ELE dashboard, the availability of which helps monitor the evolution of technological support, identify gaps for each of the languages covered, and enable cross-language comparisons.

7. Acknowledgements

The work presented in this paper has been co-financed by the European Union under grant agreement LC-01641480 – 101018166 (European Language Equality). Part of the work has also been supported by the European Union's Horizon 2020 research and innovation programme under grant agreement no. 825627 (European Language Grid).

8. Bibliographical References

Albertoni, R., D. Browning, S. Cox, A. Gonzalez-Beltran, A. Perego, and P. Winstanley (Eds.) (2020). Data Catalog Vocabulary (DCAT) - Version 2. W3C. https://www.w3.org/TR/vocab-dcat-2/.

Alemu, G., B. Stevens, and P. Ross (2012). Towards a conceptual framework for user-driven semantic metadata interoperability in digital libraries: a social constructivist approach. *New Library World*, vol. 113, no. 1/2.

Broeder, Daan, Trippel, Thorsten, Degl'Innocenti, Emiliano, Giacomi, Roberta, Sanesi, Maurizio, Kleemola, Mari, Moilanen, Katja, Ala-Lahti, Henri, Jordan, Caspar, Alfredsson, Iris, L'Hours, Hervé, & Ďurčo, Matej (2019). SSHOC D3.1 Report on SSHOC (meta)data interoperability problems. Zenodo. https://doi.org/10.5281/zenodo.3569868.

Chan, L. M. & Zeng, M. L. (2006). Metadata Interoperability and Standardization - A Study of Methodology Part I: Achieving Interoperability at the Schema Level. *D-Lib Magazine*, vol. 12, no. 6. https://doi.org/10.1045/june2006-chan.

DataCite Metadata Working Group (2021). DataCite Metadata Schema Documentation for the Publication and Citation of Research Data and Other Research Outputs v4.4. https://doi.org/10.14454/3w3z-sa82.

Gaspari, F., Way, A., Dunne, J., Rehm, G., Piperidis, S., and Giagkou, M. (2021). Deliverable D1.1 - Digital Language Equality (Preliminary Definition). European Language Equality. https://european-language-equality.eu/wp-content/uploads/2021/05/ELE_Deliverable_D1_1.pdf.

Gaspari, F., Grützner-Zahn, A., Rehm, G., Gallagher, O., Piperidis. S., and Way, A. (2022). Digital Language Equality (Full Specification). European Language Equality. https://european-language-equality.eu/wp-content/uploads/2022/04/ELE___Deliverable_D1_3.pdf

Gavrilidou, M., Labropoulou, P., Desipri, E., Giannopoulou, I., Hamon, O., and Arranz, V. (2012). The META-SHARE Metadata Schema: Principles,

[33] Direct access to the dashboard: https://live.european-language-grid.eu/catalogue/dashboard

[34] https://react-chartjs-2.js.org/

[35] https://www.chartjs.org/chartjs-plugin-zoom/

Features,Implementation and Conversion from Other Schemas. In *Proceedings of LREC 2012 - Workshop on Describing Language Resources with Metadata*, Istanbul, Turkey. European Language Resources Association.

Giagkou, M., Piperidis, S., Rehm, G. and Dunne, J. (Eds.) (2022). Language Technology Support of Europe's Languages in 2020/2021. European Language Equality Project.

Hammarström, H., Forkel, R., Haspelmath, M., and Bank, S. (2021). Glottolog 4.5. Zenodo. https://doi.org/10.5281/zenodo.5772642

International Organization for Standardization (2007). Codes for the Representation of Names of Languages - Part 3: Alpha-3 Code for Comprehensive Coverage of Languages. https://www.iso.org/cms/render/live/en/sites/isoorg/contents/data/standard/03/95/39534.html (08.04.2022).

International Organization for Standardization (2017). ISO 15836-1:2017 Information and documentation - The Dublin Core metadata element set - Part 1: Core elements

Labropoulou, P., Gkirtzou, K., Gavriilidou, M., Deligiannis, M., Galanis, D., Piperidis, S. Rehm, G., Berger, M., Mapelli, V., Rigault, M., Arranz, V., Choukri, K., Backfried, G., Gómez Pérez, J. M. and Garcia Silva, A. (2020). Making Metadata Fit for Next Generation Language Technology Platforms: The Metadata Schema of the European Language Grid. In *Proceedings of the 12th Conference on Language Resources and Evaluation (LREC 2020).* Marseille, France, 2020. European Language Resources Association (ELRA).

Labropoulou, P., Galanis, D., Lempesis, A., Greenwood, M., Knoth, P., Eckart de Castilho, R., Sachtouris, S., Georgantopoulos, B., Anastasiou, L., Martziou, S., Gkirtzou, K. Manola, N. and Piperidis, S. (2018). OpenMinTeD: A Platform Facilitating Text Mining of Scholarly Content. In *WOSP 2018 Workshop Proceedings, Eleventh International Conference on Language Resources and Evaluation (LREC 2018)*, Miyazaki, Japan, 2018, pp. 7–12 European Language Resources Association.

Lagoze, C., H. Van de Sompel, M. Nelson, and S. Warner (eds.) (2002). Open Archives Initiative - Protocol for Metadata Harvesting - v.2.0. Open Archives. http://www.openarchives.org/OAI/openarchivesprotocol.html.

Library of Congress (1999). MARC 21 Format for Bibliographic Data. https://www.loc.gov/marc/bibliographic/.

Lösch, A., Mapelli, V., Piperidis, S., Vasiļjevs, A., Smal, L., Declerck, T. et al. (2018). European Language Resource Coordination: Collecting Language Resources for Public Sector Multilingual Information Management. In *Proceedings of the Eleventh International Conference on Language Resources and Evaluation (LREC 2018).* Miyazaki, Japan, May 2018 European Language Resources Association.

McCrae, J.P., Philipp Cimiano, Victor Rodríguez Doncel, Daniel Vila-Suero, Jorge Gracia, Luca Matteis, Roberto Navigli, Andrejs Abele, Gabriela Vulcu, and Paul Buitelaar (2015). Reconciling Heterogeneous Descriptions of Language Resources. In *Proceedings of the 4th Workshop on Linked Data in Linguistics: Resources and Applications*, Beijing, China. https://doi.org/10.18653/v1/W15-4205.

Phillips, A. and Davis, M. (2009). Tags for Identifying Languages RFC 5646. Internet Engineering Task Force.

Piperidis, S., Labropoulou, P., Deligiannis, M. and Giagkou, M. (2018). Managing Public Sector Data for Multilingual Applications Development. In *Proceedings of the Eleventh International Conference on Language Resources and Evaluation (LREC 2018)* Miyazaki, Japan. European Language Resources Association.

Rehm, G., and Uszkoreit, H. (Eds.) (2012). META-NET White Paper Series: Europe's Languages in the Digital Age. Springer.

Rehm, G., Berger, M., Elsholz, E., Hegele, S., Marheinecke, K., Piperidis, S., et al. (2020). European Language Grid: An Overview. In *Proceedings of the 12th Conference on Language Resources and Evaluation (LREC 2020).* Marseille, France, 2020. European Language Resources Association.

Rehm, G., Piperidis, S., Bontcheva, K., Hajic, J., Arranz, V., Vasiļjevs, A., et al. (2021). European Language Grid: A Joint Platform for the European Language Technology Community. In *Proceedings of the 16th Conference of the European Chapter of the Association for Computational Linguistics: System Demonstrations, Online,* April 2021, pp. 221–230 Association for Computational Linguistics.

Soria, C., Núria Bel, Khalid Choukri, Joseph Mariani, Monica Monachini, Jan Odijk, Stelios Piperidis, Valeria Quochi, and Nicoletta Calzolari (2012). The FLaReNet Strategic Language Resource Agenda. In *Proceedings of the Eighth International Conference on Language Resources and Evaluation (LREC'12)*, Istanbul, Turkey. European Language Resources Association (ELRA).

Wolf, T., Debut, L., Sanh, V., Chaumond, J., Delangue, C., Moi, A., Cistac, P., Rault, T., Louf, R., Funtowicz, M., et al. (2019). Huggingface's transformers: State-of-the-art natural language processing. ArXiv preprint arXiv:1910.03771.

Zeng, M.L. & Chan, L.M. (2006) Metadata Interoperability and Standardization - A Study of Methodology Part II: Achieving Interoperability at the Record and Repository Levels. D-Lib Magazine, vol. 12, no. 6. https://doi.org/10.1045/june2006-zeng.

9. Language Resource References

Labropoulou, P., Gkirtzou, K., Gavriilidou, M., Deligiannis, M., Galanis, D., Piperidis, S. et al. (2022). ELG-SHARE metadata schema, v3.0.1. https://gitlab.com/european-language-grid/platform/ELG-SHARE-schema.

Labropoulou, P., Aubin, S., Galanis, D., Giagkou, M., Gkirtzou, K., Knoth, P., Piperidis, S., Villegas, M., Eckart de Castilho, R. (2022). OMTD-SHARE ontology, v2.0.0 (pre-release). http://w3id.org/meta-share/omtd-share/.

Appendix: Additional figures

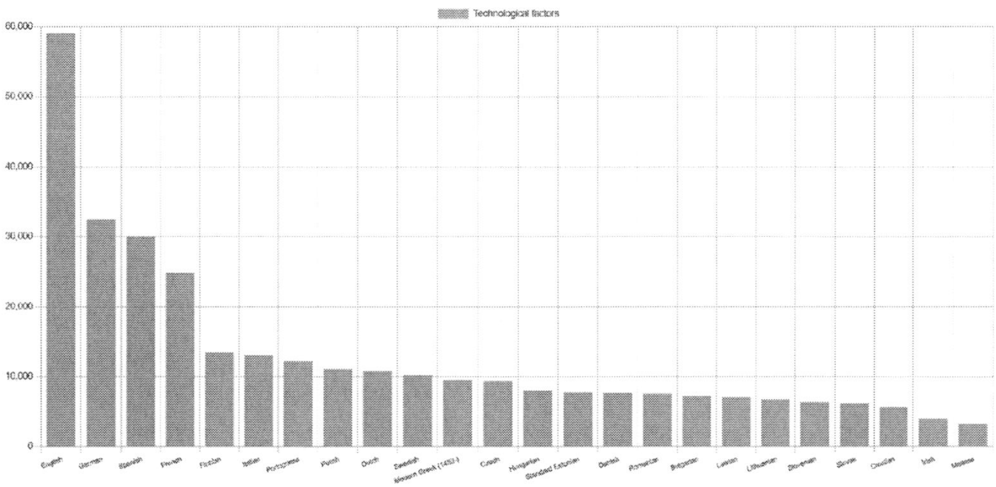

Figure 4. ELE dashboard screenshot: Technological DLE scores for the official EU languages (23 May 2022)

Proceedings of the TDLE Workshop @LREC2022, pages 36–45
Marseille, 20 June 2022

Measuring HLT Research Equality of European Languages

Gorka Artola, German Rigau
HiTZ Basque Center for Language Technologies - Ixa
University of the Basque Country UPV/EHU
{gorka.artola, german.rigau}@ehu.eus

Abstract

This work explores quantitative indicators that could potentially measure the equality and inequality research levels among the languages of the European Union in the field of human language technologies (HLT research equality). Our ultimate goal is to investigate European language equality in HLT research considering the number of papers published on several HLT research venues that mention each language with respect to their estimated number of speakers. This way, inequalities affecting HLT research in Europe will depend on other factors such as history, political status, GDP, level of social or technological development, etc. We have identified several groups of EU languages in the proposed measurement of HLT research equality, each group comprising languages with large differences in the number of speakers. We have discovered a relative equality among surprisingly different languages in terms of number of speakers and also reAll data and code will be released upon acceptance.

Keywords: human language technologies, equality, European languages

1. Introduction

The language landscape in the European Union (EU) comprises 24 official EU Member State languages, including three different alphabets, and more than 60 regional and minority languages (Pastor, 2018), including languages of relevant trade partners and immigrant communities. The fact that several of the regional languages enjoy the same level of official status as the corresponding EU Member State language in their respective regions, e.g., Aranese, Basque, Catalan, Galician, Luxembourgish, Scottish Gaelic and Welsh, and also the fact that different levels of protection by local authorities have been developed across Europe for several non-official regional or minority languages, are both European particularities not easily found in other societies in the world. One of the reasons for this diversity and public support is that multilingualism is one of the core values of the EU based on the motto 'United in diversity', and a matter deeply embedded even in the most basic regulation of the EU. A remarkable example of this can be seen in the Article 165(2) of the Treaty on the Functioning of the EU (TFEU)[1], which emphasises that *Union action shall be aimed at developing the European dimension in education, particularly through the teaching and dissemination of the languages of the Member States, while fully respecting cultural and linguistic diversity (Article 165(1) TFEU)*. Thus, for instance, the EU works with Member States to protect minorities, on the basis of the Council of Europe's European Charter for Regional or Minority Languages[2], or to promote multilingualism in the development of the EU Digital Single Market. The EU resolution "Regional and lesser-used languages - enlargement and cultural diversity"[3] is another relevant example of the subject.

A wide diversity of languages in Europe are expected to coexist, interact and evolve efficiently as equals. The strength of the multilingual EU is therefore believed to be based on the equality among European languages, but protecting and promoting language diversity, and gaining as a consequence a recognisable equality among languages operating simultaneously in a society is not an easy endeavour. The challenge is even more complex when, like in the case of the EU, the society is a conglomerate of smaller regional societal bodies with high levels of interaction and interdependence among them, but each one with a different profile and mix of coexisting languages.

The sources of inequalities among languages are multiple and possibly related to almost any dimension of its human and social condition. Economy, demography, history, geography, religion, policy and a long *etcetera* shape each and every language, making their comparison very complex. Language equality is a vibrant and remarkable challenge, and a research field that is building its own foundations. This work intends to contribute to both the European challenge and the emerging research field through the deliberation about the equality of European languages in their digital facet, particularly in the field of research in Human Language Technologies (HLT research equality).

In addition, the HLT community is currently developing powerful new deep learning techniques and tools that are revolutionizing the approach to HLT tasks. We are gradually moving from a methodology in which a pipeline of multiple modules was the typical way to im-

[1] `http://data.europa.eu/eli/treaty/tfeu_2012/oj`

[2] `https://www.coe.int/en/web/european-charter-regional-or-minority-languages`

[3] `https://www.europarl.europa.eu/doceo/document/TA-5-2003-0372_EN.html`

plement HLT solutions, to architectures based on complex neural networks trained with vast amounts of text data. The success in HLT has been possible because of the confluence of four different research trends: 1) mature deep neural network technology, 2) large amounts of data (and for NLP processing large and diverse multilingual textual data), 3) increase in High Performance Computing (HPC) power in the form of GPUs, and 4) application of simple but effective self-learning approaches. Interestingly, the application of zero-shot to few-shot transfer learning with multilingual pretrained language models, prompt learning and self-supervised systems opens up the way to leverage HLT for less developed languages (Goodfellow et al., 2016; Devlin et al., 2019; Liu et al., 2020; Torfi et al., 2020; Wolf et al., 2020). However, a growing concern is that due to unequal access to these resources only certain IT companies and elite universities have advantages in modern HLT research (Ahmed and Wahed, 2020).

After this introduction, Section 2 presents several studies carried out on language equality. Sections 3 and 4 describe our research framework and Section 5 provides an in-depth analysis of the HLT research equality of the European languages on the basis of the quantitative indicators proposed in this work. Finally, Section 6 summarizes our main findings and presents our future work.

2. Related work

Given the role of HLT in everyone's daily lives, many expert practitioners are directly concerned by language diversity in HLT research and development.[4] For instance, Sayers et al. (2021) emphasise a range of groups who will be disadvantaged. Looking ahead, they see many intriguing opportunities and new capabilities, but also a range of other sources of uncertainties and inequalities. Joshi et al. (2020) examine the relation between the types of languages, resources and their representation in NLP conferences over time. As expected, only a very small number of the over 7000 languages of the world are represented in the rapidly evolving HLT field. Just a handful of languages are covered by current NLP systems, drawn from a few dominant language families. As a result, most linguistic phenomena from typologically diverse languages have never been incorporated to our HLT research (Ponti et al., 2019). Blasi et al. (2021) study the systematic inequalities in HLT across World languages. After English, a handful of Western European Languages dominate the field -in particular German, Spanish and French- as well as even fewer non-Indo-European languages, primarily Chinese, Japanese and Arabic. This investigation suggests that it is the economy of the users of a language (rather than demography) what drives the development of HLT.

While language diversity is at the core of Europe identity and multilingual society, many of our languages are in danger of digital extinction because they are not sufficiently supported through HLT (Moseley, 2010). The EUROMAP Language Technologies was the first project investigating the state-of-the-art of HLT research and take-up in Europe, as well as the background situation in each country (Joscelyne and Lockwood, 2003). *META-NET White Paper Series: Europe's Languages in the Digital Age* (Rehm and Uszkoreit, 2012; Rehm et al., 2014) provide the first systematic study about the technology support of Europe's languages. The Rehm and Hegele (2018) survey represents the voices of more than 600 respondents from more than 50 countries working on LT. Rehm et al. (2020) present an overview of various European HLT and AI reports, and perform an extensive qualitative analysis of the landscape of research on HLT research in all the Member countries of the EU.

Both works of Joshi et al. (2020) and Blasi et al. (2021) consider and use in their studies the number of papers mentioning each language as an element, among many others, to measure inequalities in HLT. Both conclude that the main European languages are among the most equal and best represented languages in HLT, considering the large-grained scope of the 7,000 estimated languages in the world. Our work intends to explore the potential of simple indicators based also on the numbers of papers mentioning each language to measure fine-grained inequalities in HLT research, and complement with quantitative data the qualitative study on European HLT research of Rehm et al. (2020). We believe that this approach could unveil inequalities not easily demonstrable by other means, that are undermining the European language diversity protection goal, and will help identify relatively low-resourced and endangered languages in HLT research even within the theoretically strongest ones.

The work in progress in the European Language Equality Project (ELE)[5] is also worth to be noted. With a large and all-encompassing consortium consisting of 52 partners covering all EU Countries, research and industry and all major pan-European initiatives, ELE develops a strategic research, innovation and implementation agenda as well as a roadmap for achieving full digital language equality in Europe by 2030.

3. Initial hypothesis

Research, development and innovation in HLT is, generally, affordable and accessible for societies that have reached certain level of human and economic development. This is believed to be the case of the Countries and Regions comprising the EU, and together with the recognition and protection levels that the EU and member states offer to the variety of European languages

[4] https://gitlab.com/ceramisch/eacl21diversity/-/wikis/EACL-2021-language-diversity-panel

[5] https://european-language-equality.eu/

creates a unique case of theoretical favourable environment for equality among these different languages.

The initial hypothesis of this work is that, particularly in the field of HLT research, the languages of the EU should show a relevant degree of equality and that any inequality must respond to other factors than technological, social, cultural or regulatory barriers. The identification of the eventual inequality among European languages in this field may lead to effective direct intervention by the stakeholders (policy makers, academy, industry and any other) that could have legitimate interest in correcting the divergence. Also, on the other hand, it could confirm the effectiveness of existing scientific, regulatory, policy and societal dynamics in the purpose of achieving the language equality.

Finally, the focus of our study in HLT research is expected to be further beneficial contributing to the general goal of language equality, provided these technologies have precisely the ability to potentially reduce inequalities among languages through the use of digital technologies. An endangered language, or a language not reaching sufficient equality with others, may converge faster to equality taking advantage of HLT research, but failing or performing poorly on it may be an unbridgeable barrier to gain overall language equality, or even a menace towards the ongoing digital transformation.

4. Selected Languages, Data Sources and Measurement Indicators

For the identification, denomination and basic characterisation of European Languages involved in the study, and also for the estimation of the number of speakers in Europe for each language, we have followed the criteria designed by the previously mentioned European Language Equality Project (ELE). The selection of the source of data itself introduces a certain degree of a bias, particularly in non-official languages or in cases of very few speakers, on which there is no consensus denominating the language or the speaker statistics, and this will be taken into account in the analysis of the results.

We make the working assumption that a mention of a language in a research paper likely entails that the underlying research involves in some extent this language, that the more the papers mentioning a particular language the more the chance that HLT research is having a positive impact on that language, and the better is its position in the field of HLT research. Of course, we do not pretend this to be a measure of the overall HLT equality between languages, but just a measure of the presence of each language in HLT research.

The first basic indicator we have selected to explore the quantitative measurement the equality among languages in the field of HLT research is the number of scientific documents that mention each language published in the period from 2000 to 2020. We will refer to this measurement as the *absolute metric*. Not being feasible to gather and analyse the whole global scientific production in this field, we have selected a group of relevant venues and sources where the most relevant scientific documents of the field are most likely to have been published. These selected sources are the Proceedings of the bi-anual Language Resources and Evaluation Conference (LREC)[6], the Annual Meeting of the Association for Computational Linguistics (ACL)[7], the Conference on Empirical Methods in Natural Language Processing (EMNLP)[8], and the Computational Linguistics Journal (CL)[9]. The selection of these publication venues also introduces a bias to be taken into account in any analysis of these measurements. We have crawled all documents in pdf format published in these venues from 2000 to 2020 available in the ACL Anthology website[10], computationally extracted the text of these files transforming them in plain text files, and found what EU languages are mentioned in each document, according to the list developed by the ELE project[11]. Proper names that are the same as EU languages but not refer to a Language, e.g. "Basque" in the name "University of the Basque Country", have also been detected and not included in the counts of language mentions. Table 1 shows the number of research papers processed from each source.

Source	Papers
LREC	7,175
ACL	9,672
EMNLP	7,087
CL	1,977
Total	25,911

Table 1: Number of processed research papers per source

As a second quantitative measurement of HLT research equality, we propose to compare also the number of documents mentioning each language per million of speakers. We will refer to this indicator as the *relative metric*. The rationale behind the proposal of this indicator is an attempt to remove from the analysis the effect that plain demography may have in HLT research. Between two hypothetical languages where all variables affecting them could be considered exactly the same with the exception of the number of speakers, it would be reasonable to expect to have more researchers in HLT in the most spoken one of them, and also more likely that they mention their own language in the scientific production. Thus, in the extent the *ab-*

[6]https://aclanthology.org/venues/lrec/

[7]https://aclanthology.org/venues/acl/

[8]https://aclanthology.org/venues/emnlp/

[9]https://aclanthology.org/venues/cl/

[10]https://aclanthology.org/

[11]https://european-language-equality.eu/languages/

solute metric has no capacity to give information about this subject we have considered the need to introduce this second metric.

5. Analysis of language equality

As a starting reference point, Figure 1 describes, the breakdown of the number of estimated speakers in the EU for the languages of the EU considered in the ELE project sorted by the share of each language in the total. Around 80% of speakers are concentrated in 8 languages out of 67 main EU languages. This top group includes three of what we could define as "global" languages, English, Spanish and Portuguese, languages born in Europe but with more speakers abroad than in their countries of origin. Similarly, 75% of the speakers concerned by the top 8 languages are concentrated in only three languages (English, German, French). Considering only this demographic metric, languages of the EU are inherently and deeply non equal.

Figure 2 shows the breakdown of European languages sorted by total number of documents mentioning each language in the sources selected for the study. If we take this *absolute metric* as a measurement of the HLT research equality of European languages, this figure shows a high degree of overall inequality in this field, but comparing this figure with Figure 1 we may consider groups of languages with some extent of equality on HLT research within the global intrinsic inequality. English grows remarkably, comparatively to all the rest in this metric, but German and French seem to reduce and appear closer to the position of Spanish and Italian. Similarly, Dutch, Czech, Swedish, Portuguese and Turkish also grow with respect to their relative sizes in Figure 1. Maybe the most remarkable advancements in ranking are those of Turkish and Portuguese, languages that like English are, in addition to European Languages, National Official languages of very large countries outside Europe like Turkey, Brazil, etc. We can also observe that, while Greek seems to maintain its position, other strong languages in Europe like Romanian, Hungarian and Polish in terms of number of speaker loose ground compared to less spoken languages. These variations in the relative position of each language in these rankings suggest that there could be HLT research equality and inequality clusters of different nature among European languages, not affecting only low-resource and endangered languages but also some of the most spoken languages and National Official languages in Europe.

Figure 3 shows the breakdown of the number of documents mentioning each language per million of speakers of that language in Europe. We have removed from this ranking languages below 100.000 speakers to avoid introducing non representative distortions in the comparison with languages with several millions of speakers. Observing the pie chart, and comparing it to the ones in figures 1 and 2, we can observe that, according to this *relative metric*, the differences between languages are lower showing higher overall HLT research equality levels among EU languages. At a first glance, now the most spoken and most mentioned languages rank in middle to lower positions in the list, and on the contrary, some languages with lower numbers of speakers like Basque, Icelandic and Breton rise to the top of the list. Remarkably, Turkish also appears in top position despite being a language received in Europe through immigration. But also in this case, we can observe different circumstances among languages. With this metric we can observe HLT research inequalities within the group of less spoken, potentially endangered languages. We can observe some of these languages in

Figure 1: Proportion of speakers in the EU per language of the EU.

Figure 2: Proportion of documents mentioning languages of the EU (only languages with published documents).

Figure 3: Proportion of documents mentioning languages of the EU per million of speakers (only languages with published documents and with over 100.000 speakers in the EU).

the top positions in the chart, and also some of them in the lowest positions, evidencing a particular kind of inequality in HLT research in European languages, the ones that rank in lower positions both in the *absolute metric* and the *relative metric*.

Table 2 includes the EU languages identified in the ELE project for which no mentions have been found in the HLT research publications. We find in this table eight languages classified by the ELE project as Additional Languages and four Endangered Languages spoken in Europe, and none of them happens to enjoy any officially recognised status by the regional governments of the areas where they are spoken.[12] The presence of Southern Italian, with 5,700,000 estimated speakers, and less spoken but still relevant languages like Lezghin and Réunion Creole in this list suggests existence of weaknesses of some nature around these languages and HLT research. Anyhow, this list brings to surface the potential existence of a group of EU lan-

[12]It is also possible that some research papers identify these languages with other names than the ones given in the ELE project, or that HLT research on these languages is published on venues not included in this study.

ELE language	ELE Classification	Speakers
Southern Italian	Additional Languages spoken in Europe	5,700,000
Lezghin	Additional Languages spoken in Europe	600,000
Réunion Creole	Additional Languages spoken in Europe	484,000
Franco Provencal	Endangered Languages spoken in Europe	227,000
Carpato-Rusyn	Additional Languages spoken in Europe	135,810
Arberesh	Endangered Languages spoken in Europe	100,000
Plattdeutsch	Additional Languages spoken in Europe	90,000
Tornedalian Finnish	Additional Languages spoken in Europe	30,000
Jèrriais	Endangered Languages spoken in Europe	18,700
Carpathian-German	Additional Languages spoken in Europe	4,690
Mocheno	Endangered Languages spoken in Europe	1,900
Meskhetian	Additional Languages spoken in Europe	200

Table 2: EU languages not found in LREC, ACL, EMNLP and CL documents (2000-2020)

guages suffering from an extreme HLT research inequality including theoretically non endangered languages with a relevant number of speakers.

Table 3 included in the Appendix shows the EU languages ordered in decreasing number of the total sum of LREC, ACL, EMNLP and CL papers between 2000-2020 mentioning each language. Interestingly, all the three venues and the journal publish research papers that mention many different languages in quite similar distributions. Both tables 2 and 3 also show the classification given to each language in the ELE project regarding if they are Official EU Languages, Additional Languages spoken in Europe or Endangered Languages spoken in Europe. In the second and third of these groups, Additional or Endangered Languages, we can find official languages of non EU Member States like Norwegian or Turkish, co-official languages of European Regions like Frisian (Additional) or Scottish Gaelic (Endangered), languages with certain recognition in their respective regions despite not being co-official like Venetian (Additional) or Breton (Endangered), and languages with no official status or recognition at all like Sicilian (Additional) or Lombard (Endagered). It is also worth noting the presence of Catalan and Basque, co-official languages in their respective regions in the top levels of the list overtaking several Official EU languages with a bigger number of speakers. Also, Turkish as the highest ranking non EU State Official language, precedes several Official EU Languages but in this case with a remarkably higher number estimated speakers than them. Picard, Breton and Tatar, with 700,000, 206,000 and 20,550 estimated speakers respectively, are the topmost mentioned Endangered Languages in LREC, ACL, EMNLP and CL documents 2000-2020, way above of much more spoken *Aditional Languages* like Sicilian, Lombard or Venetian with 4.7 million, 3.9 million and 3.8 million estimated speakers respectively.

Figure 4 describes the evolution of the number of papers mentioning the 20 most mentioned EU languages per year in the 2000 to 2020 period, i.e., the *absolute metric*. We can observe an overall nice and relatively parallel evolution of the number of research papers mentioning each EU language, particularly in the case of the most spoken languages. From this figure we could conclude that, with the exception of English probably due to its global *lingua franca* nature, the bigger the number of European citizens living in a country where the language is official, the higher the position of the language in this characterisation HLT research equality. As expected, this *absolute* top 20 list includes some of the most spoken Official EU Languages, but also Turkish and Norwegian, languages with non official status in the EU, and Catalan and Basque, both of them *Additional Languages* spoken in Europe that enjoy full official status in their respective regions.

Figure 5 describes the evolution of the number of papers mentioning the top 20 EU languages mentioned on documents per million of estimated speakers, i.e., the *relative metric*. This *relative* top 20 list includes, as we could expect, mainly languages with lower number of speakers, some of them Official EU Languages like Estonian, Maltese, Irish, Czech, Danish, Latvian, Finnish and Slovene, and all of the rest are languages enjoying a certain degree of official status or recognition in their respective regions of reference. Also remarkably we can observe that Czech, Swedish, Norwegian, Finnish, Danish, Basque, Portuguese and Turkish are in both in the *absolute* and the *relative* top 20 language list, Basque being the only non-national Official EU Language one. It seems that the group of languages ranking in similarly high positions in both the *absolute* and the *relative metric*, also exhibits some sort of equality in HLT research among them.

Stepping a bit deeper in this *relative metric*, Figure 6 depicts the evolution of the number of research papers mentioning EU languages per million of speakers for the most spoken EU languages (over 10 million speakers in Europe) between 2000 and 2020. In this figure we can observe how languages with a lower number of estimated speakers rank consistently better than those languages with a higher number of estimated speakers. Taking English as a reference we can observe two different groups within these strongest languages. On

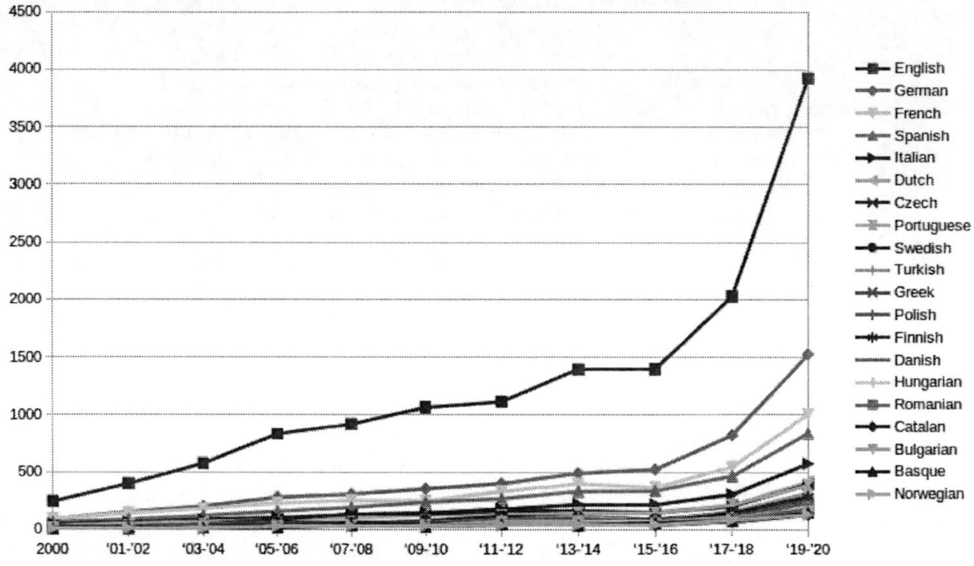

Figure 4: Evolution of mentions of European languages in LREC, ACL, EMNLP and CL documents 2000-2020.

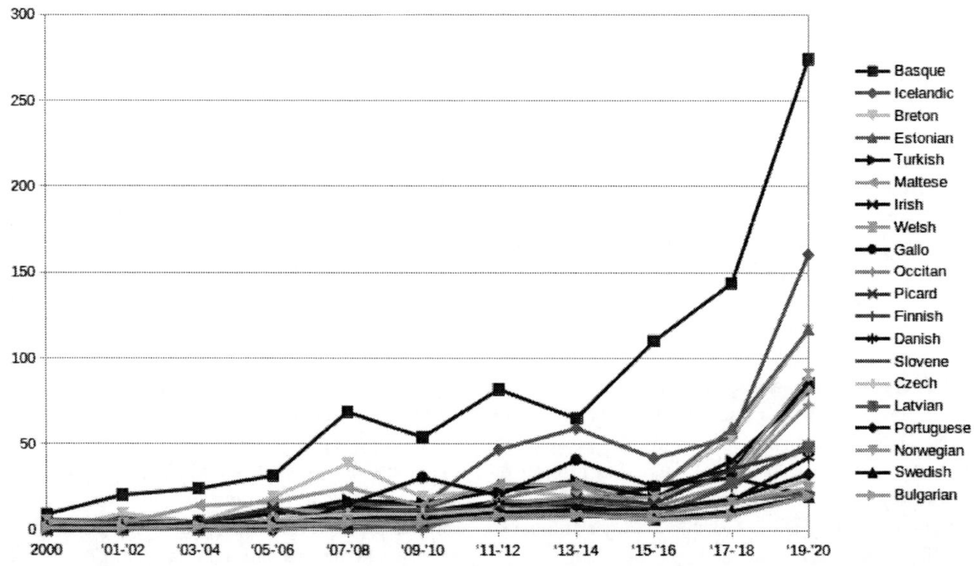

Figure 5: Evolution of mentions of European languages in LREC, ACL, EMNLP and CL documents 2000-2020 per million speakers.

one hand the ones on higher positions than English with Portuguese, Czech, Swedish, Greek, Dutch and Hungarian in this group, and those on lower positions than English with Spanish, German, Italian, Romanian, French, Serbian and Polish in this group. The existence of these two groups according to this metric may suggest the existence of a new inequality in HLT research in this case compared to the international *lingua franca*. Some strong European languages may be underrepresented and lagging too much behind English in HLT research in proportion to their demographic relevance in Europe.

6. Conclusions

This work proposes two quantitative metrics for measuring the HLT research equality of European lan-

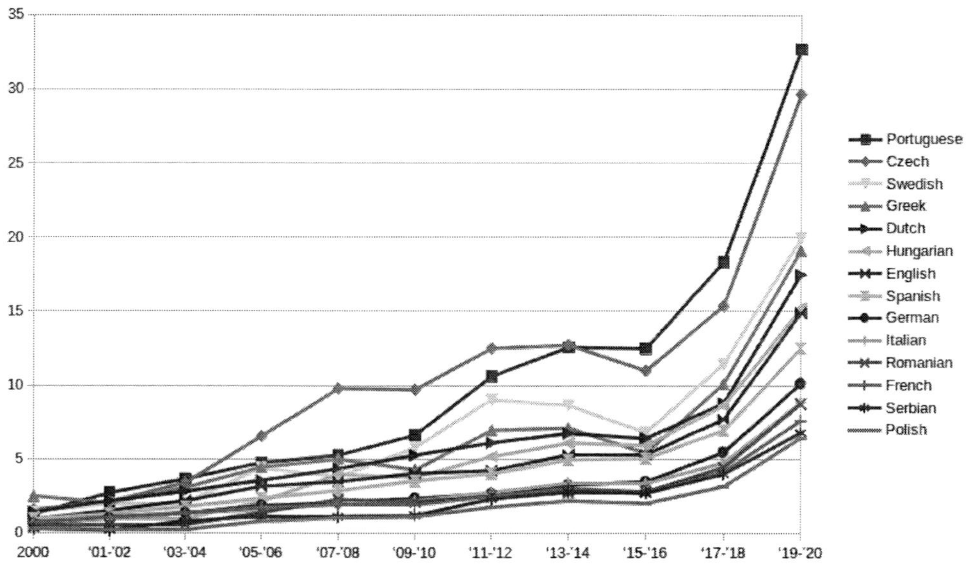

Figure 6: LREC, ACL, EMNLP and CL documents 2000-2020 mentioning the top EU languages (over 10 million speakers in the EU) per million speakers.

guages: an *absolute metric* counting the number of HLT scientific papers mentioning each language, and a *relative metric* counting the number of papers mentioning each language per million of European speakers. These two metrics do not pretend to measure the performance or effectiveness of the overall HLT research among languages.

The data gathered and analysed in this work suggests that despite the effort towards language equality of HLT research in Europe, there is still a large room for improvement. In fact, according to the proposed metrics on the selected data sources the European languages are largely unequal in HLT research. Nevertheless we have identified three groups of EU languages with a relatively homogeneous behaviour in terms of HLT research according to the proposed metrics. Each group comprises languages of quite a varying number of speakers: 1) a group of EU languages that we may describe equal in the vulnerability regarding HLT research ranking poorly in both the *absolute* and the *relative* metrics, in addition to the languages with no mention found. This group includes a long list of languages, some of them with a large number of speakers like Sicilian, Sardinian, Venetian, Alsatian Lombard or Romani; 2) a group of languages that appear in top positions in both proposed metrics and with Czech, Swedish, Norwegian, Finnish, Danish, Basque, Portuguese and Turkish as some clear representatives, and 3) a group of strong official languages with a large base of speakers ranking in a high position in the *absolute metric* and in an intermediate position in the *relative metric*, including among others German, French, Italian, Spanish and Dutch, that could be lagging behind English for its outstanding position in the *absolute metric*. There are of course also languages in intermediate positions between these groups.

As expected, we have observed that the combination of officialdom and a relevant number of speakers are positive conditions for a higher presence in HLT research. Also, not being a recognized language, at least regionally, burdens definitely its equality with respect to the ones that enjoy some degree of officialdom, no matter the size of the population speaking that language. On the other hand, it seems that regionally recognised languages can perform as good as national Official EU Languages.

Finally, we can conclude that the combination of both indicators can be of utility for measuring the HLT research equality.

Next, we plan to set up a dashboard web site to interact and order the data by its different parameters. Additionally, we plan to perform an in-depth analysis of the sources of inequalities for a better future support and understanding of the HLT research equality in Europe and other multilingual regions in the world.[13]

7. Bibliographical References

Ahmed, N. and Wahed, M. (2020). The de-democratization of ai: Deep learning and the compute divide in artificial intelligence research. *arXiv preprint arXiv:2010.15581*.

Blasi, D., Anastasopoulos, A., and Neubig, G. (2021). Systematic inequalities in language technology per-

[13]The data and code will be released upon acceptance.

formance across the world's languages. *arXiv e-prints*, pages arXiv–2110.

Devlin, J., Chang, M.-W., Lee, K., and Toutanova, K. (2019). BERT: Pre-training of deep bidirectional transformers for language understanding. In *Proceedings of the 2019 Conference of the North American Chapter of the Association for Computational Linguistics: Human Language Technologies, Volume 1 (Long and Short Papers)*, pages 4171–4186, Minneapolis, Minnesota. Association for Computational Linguistics.

Goodfellow, I. J., Bengio, Y., and Courville, A. (2016). *Deep Learning*. MIT Press, Cambridge, MA, USA.

Joscelyne, A. and Lockwood, R. (2003). *Benchmarking HLT progress in Europe*. EUROMAP Language Technologies, Center for Sprogteknologi.

Joshi, P., Santy, S., Budhiraja, A., Bali, K., and Choudhury, M. (2020). The state and fate of linguistic diversity and inclusion in the NLP world. In *Proceedings of the 58th Annual Meeting of the Association for Computational Linguistics*, pages 6282–6293, Online, July. Association for Computational Linguistics.

Liu, Y., Gu, J., Goyal, N., Li, X., Edunov, S., Ghazvininejad, M., Lewis, M., and Zettlemoyer, L. (2020). Multilingual denoising pre-training for neural machine translation. *Transactions of the Association for Computational Linguistics*, 8:726–742.

Moseley, C. (2010). Atlas of the world's languages in danger, 3rd edn.

Pastor, R. (2018). *Language equality in the digital age : towards a human language project*. European Parliament.

Ponti, E. M., O'Horan, H., Berzak, Y., Vulić, I., Reichart, R., Poibeau, T., Shutova, E., and Korhonen, A. (2019). Modeling Language Variation and Universals: A Survey on Typological Linguistics for Natural Language Processing. *Computational Linguistics*, 45(3):559–601, 09.

Rehm, G. and Hegele, S. (2018). Language technology for multilingual Europe: An analysis of a large-scale survey regarding challenges, demands, gaps and needs. In *Proceedings of the Eleventh International Conference on Language Resources and Evaluation (LREC 2018)*, Miyazaki, Japan. European Language Resources Association (ELRA).

Georg Rehm et al., editors. (2012). *META-NET White Paper Series: Europe's Languages in the Digital Age*, 32 volumes on 31 European languages, Heidelberg etc. Springer.

Rehm, G., Uszkoreit, H., Dagan, I., Goetcherian, V., Dogan, M. U., Mermer, C., Váradi, T., Kirchmeier-Andersen, S., Stickel, G., Jones, M. P., Oeter, S., and Gramstad, S. (2014). An Update and Extension of the META-NET Study "Europe's Languages in the Digital Age". In Laurette Pretorius, et al., editors, *Proceedings of the Workshop on Collaboration and Computing for Under-Resourced Languages in the Linked Open Data Era (CCURL 2014)*, pages 30–37, Reykjavik, Iceland.

Rehm, G., Marheinecke, K., Hegele, S., Piperidis, S., Bontcheva, K., Hajič, J., Choukri, K., Vasiļjevs, A., Backfried, G., Prinz, C., Gómez-Pérez, J. M., Meertens, L., Lukowicz, P., van Genabith, J., Lösch, A., Slusallek, P., Irgens, M., Gatellier, P., Köhler, J., Le Bars, L., Anastasiou, D., Auksoriūtė, A., Bel, N., Branco, A., Budin, G., Daelemans, W., De Smedt, K., Garabík, R., Gavriilidou, M., Gromann, D., Koeva, S., Krek, S., Krstev, C., Lindén, K., Magnini, B., Odijk, J., Ogrodniczuk, M., Rögnvaldsson, E., Rosner, M., Pedersen, B., Skadiņa, I., Tadić, M., Tufiș, D., Váradi, T., Vider, K., Way, A., and Yvon, F. (2020). The European language technology landscape in 2020: Language-centric and human-centric AI for cross-cultural communication in multilingual Europe. In *Proceedings of the 12th Language Resources and Evaluation Conference*, pages 3322–3332, Marseille, France. European Language Resources Association.

Sayers, D., Sousa-Silva, R., Höhn, S., Ahmedi, L., Allkivi-Metsoja, K., Anastasiou, D., Beňuš, Štefan; Bowker, L., Bytyçi, E., Catala, A., Çepani, A., Chacón-Beltrán, Rubén; Dadi, S., Dalipi, F., Despotovic, V., Doczekalska, A., Drude, S., Fort, Karën; Fuchs, R., Galinski, C., Galinski, C., Galinski, C., Gobbo, F., Gungor, T., Guo, S., Höckner, K., Láncos, P., Libal, T., Jantunen, T., Jones, D., Klimova, B., Korkmaz, E., Maučec, M. S., Melo, M., Meunier, F., Migge, B., Mititelu, V. B., Névéol, Aurélie; Rossi, A., Pareja-Lora, A., Sanchez-Stockhammer, C.; Şahin, A., Soltan, A., Soria, C., Shaikh, S., Turchi, M., Yildirim Yayilgan, S., Bessa, M., Cabral, L., Coler, M., Liebeskind, C., Kernerman, I., Rousi, R., and Prys, C. (2021). The dawn of the human-machine era : A forecast of new and emerging language technologies. Technical report, LITHME project.

Torfi, A., Shirvani, R. A., Keneshloo, Y., Tavvaf, N., and Fox, E. A. (2020). Natural language processing advancements by deep learning: A survey. *arXiv preprint arXiv:2003.01200*.

Wolf, T., Debut, L., Sanh, V., Chaumond, J., Delangue, C., Moi, A., Cistac, P., Rault, T., Louf, R., Funtowicz, M., Davison, J., Shleifer, S., von Platen, P., Ma, C., Jernite, Y., Plu, J., Xu, C., Le Scao, T., Gugger, S., Drame, M., Lhoest, Q., and Rush, A. (2020). Transformers: State-of-the-art natural language processing. In *Proceedings of the 2020 Conference on Empirical Methods in Natural Language Processing: System Demonstrations*, pages 38–45, Online. Association for Computational Linguistics.

Appendix

Language	Classification	Speakers	LREC	ACL	EMNLP	CL	Total
English	Official European Union Languages	263,835,370	4,676	4,839	3,837	531	13,883
German	Official European Union Languages	150,888,580	2,013	1,602	1,304	227	5,146
French	Official European Union Languages	131,992,030	1,783	1,027	803	182	3,795
Spanish	Official European Union Languages	67,144,190	1,377	872	723	131	3,103
Italian	Official European Union Languages	65,019,690	1,004	554	429	87	2,074
Dutch	Official European Union Languages	23,918,840	737	423	310	86	1,556
Czech	Official European Union Languages	13,295,420	593	510	361	55	1,519
Portuguese	Official European Union Languages	11,787,500	627	358	269	53	1,307
Swedish	Official European Union Languages	12,947,670	449	267	209	49	974
Turkish	Additional Languages spoken in Europe	3,905,040	302	342	261	62	967
Greek	Official European Union Languages	12,399,170	391	221	206	49	867
Polish	Official European Union Languages	39,415,080	353	220	153	32	758
Finnish	Official European Union Languages	5,682,630	263	267	183	32	745
Danish	Official European Union Languages	5,563,120	252	234	213	19	718
Hungarian	Official European Union Languages	12,177,260	254	219	155	28	656
Romanian	Official European Union Languages	20,776,510	265	194	114	21	594
Catalan	Additional Languages spoken in Europe	8,973,480	274	128	117	29	548
Bulgarian	Official European Union Languages	7,570,230	212	173	122	26	533
Basque	Additional Languages spoken in Europe	536,000	191	130	133	20	474
Norwegian	Additional Languages spoken in Europe	5,254,060	208	121	102	21	452
Estonian	Official European Union Languages	1,128,990	146	104	80	13	343
Croatian	Official European Union Languages	6,590,290	160	84	64	9	317
Irish	Official European Union Languages	1,176,730	102	86	67	7	262
Slovene	Official European Union Languages	2,195,790	118	79	52	10	259
Slovak	Official European Union Languages	7,174,580	115	63	58	5	241
Serbian	Additional Languages spoken in Europe	10,025,456	112	55	61	5	233
Latvian	Official European Union Languages	1,933,100	98	64	47	9	218
Lithuanian	Official European Union Languages	2,793,100	70	76	36	3	185
Icelandic	Additional Languages spoken in Europe	404,683	85	57	20	5	167
Galician	Additional Languages spoken in Europe	2,335,000	80	45	28	2	155
Welsh	Additional Languages spoken in Europe	562,000	49	37	29	9	124
Maltese	Official European Union Languages	485,110	66	37	13	3	119
Picard	Endangered Languages spoken in Europe	700,000	36	39	35	3	113
Macedonian	Additional Languages spoken in Europe	1,553,203	40	30	16	5	91
Breton	Endangered Languages spoken in Europe	206,000	32	18	15	3	68
Tatar	Endangered Languages spoken in Europe	20,550	17	14	18	1	50
Faroese	Additional Languages spoken in Europe	76,587	23	13	13	0	49
Frisian	Additional Languages spoken in Europe	883,000	22	22	3	1	48
Sorbian	Endangered Languages spoken in Europe	19,970	16	6	24	1	47
Asturian	Endangered Languages spoken in Europe	560,000	21	13	4	0	38
Occitan	Additional Languages spoken in Europe	218,310	25	7	5	0	37
Gallo	Endangered Languages spoken in Europe	195,000	10	12	12	3	37
Romani	Endangered Languages spoken in Europe	3,755,600	14	15	7	0	36
Yiddish	Endangered Languages spoken in Europe	10,977	13	14	3	2	32
Lombard	Endangered Languages spoken in Europe	3,903,000	22	5	3	0	30
Luxembourgish	Additional Languages spoken in Europe	510,900	15	9	4	0	28
Cornish	Endangered Languages spoken in Europe	600	6	13	5	3	27
Scottish Gaelic	Endangered Languages spoken in Europe	57,400	12	4	9	1	26
Venetian	Additional Languages spoken in Europe	3,850,000	13	6	1	0	20
Aragonese	Endangered Languages spoken in Europe	30,000	8	6	3	0	17
Sardinian	Endangered Languages spoken in Europe	1,200,000	10	4	2	1	17
Ladin	Endangered Languages spoken in Europe	31,000	8	6	1	0	15
Sicilian	Additional Languages spoken in Europe	4,700,000	8	4	3	0	15
Karelian	Endangered Languages spoken in Europe	5,000	7	4	3	0	14
Saami	Endangered Languages spoken in Europe	22,430	7	3	4	0	14
Manx	Endangered Languages spoken in Europe	1,660	5	4	2	1	12
Alsatian	Additional Languages spoken in Europe	600,000	8	0	2	1	11

Table 3: Number of LREC, ACL, EMNLP and CL documents 2000-2020 mentioning EU languages (languages with over 10 documents mentioning them)

Proceedings of the TDLE Workshop @LREC2022, pages 46–51
Marseille, 20 June 2022

National Language Technology Platform for Public Administration

Marko Tadić[1], Daša Farkaš[1], Matea Filko[1], Artūrs Vasiļevskis[2], Andrejs Vasiļjevs[2], Jānis Ziediņš[3], Željka Motika[4], Mark Fishel[5], Hrafn Loftsson[6], Jón Guðnason[6], Claudia Borg[7], Keith Cortis[8], Judie Attard[8], Donatienne Spiteri[9]

[1]University of Zagreb, Faculty of Humanities and Social Sciences, Zagreb, Croatia, {marko.tadic, dasa.farkas, matea.filko}@ffzg.hr
[2]Tilde, Riga, Latvia, {arturs.vasilevskis, andrejs.vasiljevs}@tilde.com
[3]Culture Information Systems Centre, Riga, Latvia, janis.ziedins@kis.gov.lv
[4]Central State Office for the Development of Digital Society, Zagreb, Croatia, Zeljka.Motika@rdd.hr
[5]University of Tartu, Tartu, Estonia, fishel@ut.ee
[6]Reykjavik University, School of Technology, Reykjavik, Iceland, {hrafn, jg}@ru.is
[7]University of Malta, Valletta, Malta, claudia.borg@um.edu.mt
[8]Malta Information Technology Agency, Blata l-Bajda, Malta, {keith.cortis, judie.attard}@gov.mt
[9]Office of the State Advocate, Valletta, Malta, donatienne.spiteri@stateadvocate.mt

Abstract

This article presents the work in progress on the collaborative project of several European countries to develop National Language Technology Platform (NLTP). The project aims at combining the most advanced Language Technology tools and solutions in a new, state-of-the-art, Artificial Intelligence driven, National Language Technology Platform for five EU/EEA official and lower-resourced languages.

Keywords: machine translation, CAT tools, parallel corpora, National Language Technology Platform

1. Introduction

Multilingualism is one of Europe's fundamental values, alongside freedom of expression and freedom of movement. The European Charter of Fundamental Rights perpetuates the rights and freedoms of European citizens and ensures that linguistic diversity is maintained as a cornerstone of European policy. While the diversity of languages used in Europe is a true treasure, the barriers resulting from language insularity create big challenges for the cohesion of the European Union Digital Single Market[1,2] (DSM), public e-services, and public administrations. Many e-services provided by national public administrations are still available only in the official language of the respective country, which greatly restricts their access to guest workers, visitors, foreign investors and many other users who do not comprehend the local language. In case the e-services and public information are also provided in English and other languages, translation creates significant expenses and management burden.

In recent years, the European Union and member states have invested in various programmes to advance Language Technologies (LTs) as an efficient solution for breaking language barriers – from large language resoures collecting campaigns like ELRC[3], over the EC eTranslation services[4], up to establishing the common European marketplate for language technologies like ELG[5]. This has resulted in numerous LT tools, and services that have demonstrated their advantages across a wide range of national and international projects and have already proven their usefulness to public administrations. Nevertheless, their current use is limited because as individual solutions and technologies, they are used only by a particular target group, in a specific context, only in a few institutions and countries.

This paper presents the work in progress on the collaborative project of several European countries to develop *National Language Technology Platform (NLTP).*[6] The project aims to unite the most advanced LT tools and solutions developed in the CEF AT and other European and national programmes in a novel state-of-the-art, Artificial Intelligence (AI) driven software solution – NLTP. NLTP will provide national public administrations, SMEs and general public with mature, tightly integrated Machine Translation (MT) and other LT services (e.g. terminology management, translation memories, speech tools for selected languages, etc.) that will serve as an efficient way to enable multilingual access to information and public online services.

By providing essential LT support to various eGovernment services, NLTP is positioned to become an essential element of eGovernment infrastructure.

[1] https://ec.europa.eu/commission/sites/beta-political/files/dsm-factsheet_en.pdf [accessed 2020-05-16].
[2] https://ec.europa.eu/commission/presscorner/detail/en/IP_15_4919
[3] https://lr-coordination.eu
[4] https://ec.europa.eu/info/resources-partners/machine-translation-public-administrations-etranslation_en
[5] https://www.european-language-grid.eu
[6] https://www.nltp-info.eu

The structure of the paper is as follows. We describe the composition of the consortium and represented languages in Section 2, followed by a brief description of the current state of the development of LT for each language in Section 3. In Section 4, the general goals and the collection of additional language resources is explained, while in Section 5 we conclude with a discussion on the targeted users of the NLTP and the user survey.

2. Consortium and Languages

The NLTP project is implemented as a CEF Telecom Action that includes partners from five countries: Latvia, Croatia, Estonia, Iceland and Malta, and it deals with LT for their respective languages: Latvian, Croatian, Estonian, Icelandic, Maltese. The consortium is deliberately composed of at least one partner (either academic or industrial) per country, that provides the expertise in LT for its language, and usually combined with one or more partners coming from public administration. In the case of Estonia and Iceland, the sole academic partners received the role of institution consulting the public administration. The project is initiated and coordinated by the LT company Tilde. The detailed list of partners can be found at the official web page of the project[7].

The five languages involved are all official languages of their respective countries, but at the same time they represent language communities with small to moderate number of speakers, starting in total with ca. 380,000 for Icelandic up to ca. 4,900,000 for Croatian, considering also citizens in other countries as emigrants of the first generation. The position of the official languages provides a unique opportunity to advocate for the state support of the usage of LT, and that is what is expected from the partners from public administration.

3. State of LT in ELE Language Reports

In this section we present in brief the state of the development of LT that was presented in more detail in the Language Reports as deliverables within the European Language Equality (ELE) project[8]. This state of development can serve as the baseline starting point, which could be used for measuring the project's progress by the end of its duration. Also, this illustrate the different stages of LT development and relevant gaps that exist between the consortium languages, as well as their different starting points. However, for all languages involved the need of more domain specific bilingual data and persistent national infrastructure for LT is stressed. We strongly believe that NLTP could contribute to both urgent needs.

3.1 Latvia

Since 2012, when the META-NET white papers were published (Skadina et al., 2012), significant progress has been made in the development and deployment of different language resources and tools for the Latvian language. Latvian also has good support in terms of more advanced technologies, such as MT, as well as speech recognition and synthesis. At the same time, solutions involving state-of-the-art natural language understanding are not so developed. There are gaps regarding the availability, size, and technology readiness level of language resources. More models, tools, as well as computational, human, and financial resources would benefit the current state of LT for Latvian. Significant gaps were identified in monolingual and multilingual data – written, spoken, and multimodal, especially when it comes to open-data or open-access language resources. Fine-tuning domain-specific engines is also more complicated than desirable, as the current domain-specific data is insufficient and lacks substantial open-access monolingual text corpora. Overall, the current LT situation in Latvia is fragmented, but going in the positive direction and continuously improving while most areas are considered to have "fragmentary support". In the whitepaper, it was mentioned that dedicated long-term LT programs would benefit research and industrial activities, with NLTP addressing the latter.

3.2 Croatia

Technological support for Croatian has progressed in a number of LT areas compared to the state of affairs described in the META-NET White Paper (Tadić et al., 2012). Digital language resources have both increased in number and volume while they also improved in quality and variety. Resources, basic NLP tools and LT services are provided by academia, research institutes and occasionally private companies as outputs of various research projects, usually coordinated by academic institutions, predominantly funded by EU or national funds, and rarely self-funded. Some significant progress has been made with respect to available corpora and lexica, language models, text processing tools, and MT, while there is still a serious underdevelopment in the field of speech processing (both synthesis and recognition). The available datasets originate from a variety of sources and they cover several thematic domains, text types; they are available as raw or annotated; and come as monolingual, bilingual or multilingual resources. However, their individual size is lagging behind in terms of appropriateness for building large language models or robust, ready to use tools and applications.

One of the long-term intentions is to secure the presence of Croatian NLP modules in the major NLP platforms (commercial and non-commercial) such as spaCy, FreeLing, NLP Cube, TextRazor, Cloud Natural Language, Apache Open NLP, etc., in order to secure the sustainability and wider usage of LT for Croatian and, consequently, its digital language equality with other languages. The inclusion of Croatian in NLTP will certainly add to this goal.

3.3 Estonia

During the last decade some LT fields have advanced significantly and for Estonian there are better and bigger corpora of contemporary written language and bigger treebanks, but several gaps that were identified by the Meta-Net White Paper in 2012 (Liin et al., 2012) are still there: text generation is still under-developed and we lack annotated semantic resources and tools for semantics. The existing tools cover the basics of text analysis – sentence segmentation, tokenisation, morphological analysis,

[7] https://www.nltp-info.eu
[8] https://european-language-equality.eu

syntactic parsing – for standard written language. The overall quality of MT and especially of speech technologies is also quite satisfactory, but only for standard language. However, Estonian lacks both annotated data and tools for certain tasks and, as annotating data is a time- and workforce-consuming process, it can be seen as an even bigger obstacle. There are large web-crawled corpora for Estonian, but less domain-specific corpora or, if such resources exist, they are not publicly available. Accordingly, resources need to be made available – as has been done successfully in other countries – to persuade Estonian data-holders of the benefits of sharing such data sets.

Most of the work in Estonian LT is done at academic institutions and is project-based. Once the project is over, the developed resources are not updated any more. Accordingly, there is a need for an infrastructure for keeping these models and tools up-to-date once the project has ended so that Estonia can continuously benefit from that important work. The national Estonian CLARIN consortium and its participation in CLARIN ERIC will strenghten this role in future.

3.4 Iceland

Ten years ago, the META-NET White Paper Series described a serious situation for the Icelandic language. At that time, Icelandic was one of the four European languages that fell into the "weak/no support" category regarding the level of support for speech processing, MT, text analysis, and speech and text resources (Rögnvaldsson et al., 2012). This alarming situation triggered concerns and discussions among politicians in the following years, which eventually resulted in the establishment and financing of the Language Technology Programme for Icelandic (LTPI), 2019-2023 (Rögnvaldsson, 2020).

The goal of the LTPI is to make Icelandic usable in information and communication technology, by developing open-source language resources and tools. The LPTI consists of six core projects: Language Resources, NLP tools, Automatic Speech Recognition, Speech synthesis, Spell and Grammar Checking, and MT (Nikulásdóttir, 2020). Even though the LTPI is still being implemented, it has already made a very significant change to the level of language technology support for the Icelandic language, as is evident by the comprehensive listing of the deliverables found in Nikulásdóttir et al. (2022), and the CLARIN-IS repository. Nevertheless, after the LTPI ends, Icelandic will still lack various NLP tools and resources, which indeed shows the need for a continued governmental support of the LTPI (Rögnvaldsson, 2020).

The inclusion of Icelandic in NLTP fits well with the LTPI, particularly regarding the MT, Speech Recognition, and Speech synthesis core packages.

3.5 Malta

The main gaps in the development of LT for Maltese are present in three general areas: (i) tools (ii) resources and (iii) support.

As far as tools are concerned, Maltese still lacks the barest minimum required for a BLARK (Basic Language Resource Kit) as defined in (Krauwer,1998). So Maltese needs not only a solid set of building blocks that will serve to build more advanced applications, but also ready and universal access to them with the help of platforms like ELG[9]. The potential for MT is beginning to be appreciated thanks to the efforts by the EC, but more effort is required locally, beyond the limited timeframe of the NLTP project, for the necessary quality to be achieved in all the domains where it can usefully serve. This requires a concerted policy to facilitate the extraction and refinement of bilingual resources at their point of creation, i.e. public administration. Speech technology, and particularly Automatic Speech Recognition (ASR), is another priority, since it imparts a highly tangible quality to LT that makes sense to ordinary people in everyday situations. Finally, for Maltese there is also a complete lack of multimodal tools.

These days, almost all of the above tools are driven by machine learning, and thus their quality depends on the availability of suitable language resources. If intelligent multimodal and multilingual machinery that involves Maltese is expected, then appropriate multimodal and multilingual corpora are needed to train it. This requires a significant effort, which, if the resources are to faithfully reflect their inherent regional characteristics, must be developed at national level.

This evokes the third gap: support. LT has not received the kind of recognition that is normally afforded to language by various national institutions. If LT for Maltese is to thrive, it needs to be recognised as a national area of priority that requires nurturing, management and support. Most of the language resources and tools that exist today have been created opportunistically. This is a short-term expedient that creates gaps and discontinuities. Language resources and tools need to be commissioned to fit carefully identified needs, and curated on a permanent basis. This requires commitment at national level, and a serious budget, as seen in Spain, Estonia, The Netherlands and even smaller countries like Iceland (Nikulásdóttir et al., 2020). Currently, the institutions that are responsible for the Maltese language adopt a helpful stance towards LT, but have not really taken on board the commitment that is required to ensure that it flourishes and exploits its full potential.

4. NLTP Goals and Resources

In this section, we first state the general goals of NLTP, then describe the work that precedes the NLTP project and provides the background knowledge and results on which we build upon. In continuation, we describe the NLTP components and the specific needs of collecting additional language resources, with the emphasis on the parallel corpora for these five languages, that are particularly deficient with this type of language resources.

[9] https://www.european-language-grid.eu

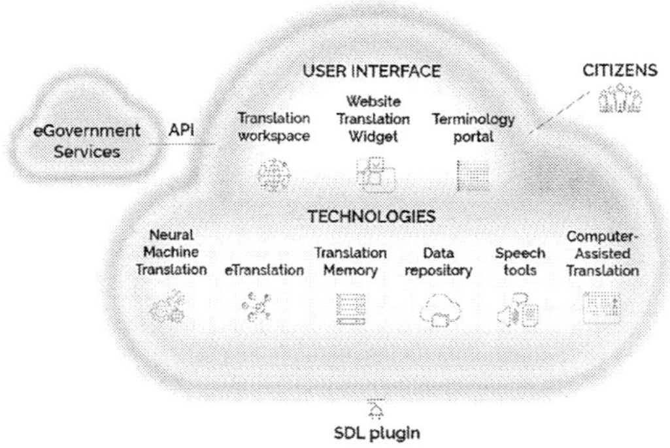

Figure 1. Schematic representation of NLTP components in the initial configuration.

4.1 General Goals

The aim of the project is to create a generic, customizable LT platform that any European country can easily adapt and deploy in their eGovernment infrastructure. The project partners are assessing the particular needs of their public administrations, tailoring the platform for their needs and deploying and integrating it into infrastructure of public digital services.

4.2 Related Work

The proposed solution for national LT platforms will rely on the existing *hugo.lv* platform[10], but it will also include the results obtained from the CEF action *EU Council Presidency Translator* (INEA/CEF/ICT/A2018/ 1762093)[11]. Both projects featured online MT services tailored for translation between the national language(s) and English in both directions. While the hugo.lv was oriented towards Latvian and English for use by Latvian public administration, the EU Council Presidency Translator covered seven languages in addition to English: Latvian, Estonian, Bulgarian, German, Romanian, Finnish and Croatian (chronologically ordered).

4.3 NLTP Components and Approach

The existing platform(s) will be substantially expanded into the planned NLTP in order to provide public administrations and the general public with a secure access to high quality MT and integration with Computer Aided Translation (CAT) tools, e-mail plug-ins, web-pages translation widgets etc., for translation of texts and documents (see Figure 1).

For both public administration and the public, this platform will be a convenient and secure environment for translating texts, documents and websites using fast and efficient newest generation Neural MT (NMT) technologies. Users will be able not only to translate entire documents in multiple languages preserving their formatting, but they can also review and edit the MT output, create and check terminology. Input and output will be either in text or voice form depending on the NLTP service provided by the consortium partners and selected by the user.

The NLTP will be adapted, localised, and sustainably deployed by the public authority bodies in the partner states as a part of the national eGovernment services and infrastructures, while its development will be supported by local research institutions as complementary partners. The inclusion of NLTP in national eGovernment infrastructures will secure the sustainability of the platform after the EU funding period.

Additionally, the NLTP will be customisable to the specific needs of each public administration. Adaptation will be carried out by redesigning the initial configuration with adapting the existing solutions developed within other projects, creating a unified and customizable user interface, and furnishing the platform with the latest neural MT (NMT) systems. NMT systems will be tailored to the specific domains of administrations using specific domain language, terminology, and communication styles. This can include legal, financial or other domains heavily used in public administration. Customization will maximize translation quality for the local languages of the hosting country.

The modular design of the NLTP allows the inclusion of other LT services when public administration express their needs for them, e.g. Automatic Speech Recognition for transcription of recorded sessions in order to produce meeting minutes, or Named Entities Recognition module in text preprocesssing step.

NLTP will be further linked to EC eTranslation services, thus enabling translations into and from the 24 official EU languages and other languages of the Digital Single Market. Equally, this platform is open for integration with other MT providers by simple integration using Docker container technology or open API connection.

The NLTP will facilitate the use of a professional translation environment with integrated terminology databases, CAT tools and (N)MT, all wrapped up in simple-to-use HTML front end and coupled with number of other technological solutions, such as a translation widget, browser plugin, commercial CAT tool plugins, etc.

4.4 Additional Resources

To customise MT systems of the platform for the domains most needed by national public administrations, a number of domain specific parallel data is being collected in all available digital formats (predominantly HTML and PDF). The processing is being done by several partners in order to reach the final targeted Translation Memory eXchange (TMX) format. The processing includes the boilerplate removal and/or PDF text extraction, automatic sentence splitting and sentence-alignment that will be checked for possible alignment errors. The bilingual language resources will be made available through the ELRC-SHARE[12] repository and other repositories. Since the sources of data are predominantly expected to come

[10] https://hugo.lv/en

[11] https://www.tilde.com/products-and-services/machine-translation/de-presidency

[12] https://elrc-share.eu

from the public domain, the data will be made accessible under permissive licences. The parallel corpora collection process will be described in a separate paper when the collection process will be completed.

5. Users

The NLTP is targeted to several target groups which are discussed in this section. In order to understand the public opinion towards the usage of LT in five countries, we have organised user surveys that are currently being run.

5.1 Targeted Users and User Requirements

The relevant stakeholders, which are expected as end-users of the platform are different bodies of public administration (local/regional/national), private sector (particularly SMEs), academia and citizens. NLTP specifications will be finally defined in collaboration with the consortium partners and relevant stakeholders using information collected in user surveys. The user groups are primarily defined through the user stories, in particular targeting user experience, i.e., defining the end-user, purpose and use of the country specific NLTP configuration. The user stories were initially defined at the project start, then updated/added accordingly during the NLTP development. The methodology for definition of user stories is based on (i) user identification and classification into group profiles, in order to place user requirements in a problem-driven context; (ii) using mock-ups of the system and its main services as a trigger in interactions with users.

The requirements are being analysed and prioritized, and the analysis will come up with the description of different types of services from the users' point of view. The requirements analysis will feed the functional specifications of the NLTP and subsequently drive the design of the architecture and its backend components.

5.2 User Survey

Targeted surveys are being run in the NLTP consortium member states with the intent to gain insight into current use, current needs, and potential future needs of the NLTP end-users and different public institutions which are adopting the NLTP concept. The surveys are being disseminated by the consortium representatives of each country through established network of contacts and responses are collected from public institutions as possible adopters and end-users. The data will be processed to identify gaps in language tools that the NLTP could fill, as well as other features that institutions in each country might benefit from. The survey results will also be used for preparation of national seminars and workshops that will promote the benefits of frequent LT usage.

6. Conclusions

We presented the NLTP, a project which aims to build a National Language Technology Platform in five EU/EEA countries intended for use primarily by public administration. The platform will initially offer what is needed the most by this category of users: the access to NMT systems (proprietary and eTranslation-based), to CALL environment in simple HTML interface, to terminology and translation memory management, but also to other LT services due to the platform's modular design.

Acknowledgements

The work reported here was supported by the European Commission in the CEF Telecom Programme (Action No: 2020-EU-IA-0082, Grant Agreement No: INEA/CEF/ICT/A2020/2278398).

References

Krauwer, S. (1998) ELSNET and ELRA: Common past, common future, *ELRA Newsletter*, Vol 3 no 2. [http://www.elsnet.org/dox/blark.html]

Liin, K., Muischnek, K., Müürisep, K. and Vider, K. (2012) *Eesti keel digiajastul – The Estonian Language in the Digital Age.* META-NET White Paper Series: Europe's Languages in Digital Age. Springer, Heidelberg, New York, Dordrecht, London. [http://www.meta-net.eu/whitepapers/volumes/estonian].

Motika, Ž., Didak Prekpalaj, T., Horvat Klemen, T., Košćec Perić, M. (in press). Predstavljanje projekta "Nacionalna platforma za jezične tehnologije" In: *Proceedings of the μPro2022 Conference*, Opatija, May 2022.

Muischnek, K. (2022) *D1.12: Report on the Estonian Language.* European Language Equality. [https://european-language-equality.eu/wp-content/uploads/2022/03/ELE___Deliverable_D1_12__Language_Report_Estonian_.pdf]

Nikulásdóttir A. B., Arnardóttir, Þ., Barkarson, S., Guðnason J., Gunnarsson, Þ. D., Ingason, A. K., Jónsson, H. P., Loftsson, H., Óladóttir, H., Rögnvaldsson, E., Sigurðsson, E. F., Sigurgeirsson, A. F., Snæbjarnarson, V., Steingrímsson, S., and Örnólfsson, G. T. (2020) Help Yourself from the Buffet: National Language Technology Infrastructure Initiative on CLARIN-IS. In *Selected Papers from the CLARIN Annual Conference.*

Nikulásdóttir A. B., Guðnason J., Ingason, A. K., Loftsson, H., Rögnvaldsson, E., Sigurðsson, E. F., and Steingrímsson, S. (2020) Language Technology Programme for Icelandic 2019-2023. In *Proceedings of the 12th International Conference on Language Resources and Evaluation (LREC 2020).*

Rögnvaldsson, E., Jóhannsdóttir, K. M., Helgadóttir, S., and Steingrímsson, S. (2012) *Íslensk tunga á stafrænni öld - The Icelandic Language in the Digital Age.* META-NET White Paper Series: Europe's Languages in the Digital Age. Springer, Heidelberg, New York, Dordrecht, London. [http://www.meta-net.eu/whitepapers/volumes/icelandic]

Rögnvaldsson, E. (2022) *D1.19: Report on the Icelandic Language.* European Language Equality. [https://european-language-equality.eu/wp-content/uploads/2022/03/ELE___Deliverable_D1_19__Language_Report_Icelandic_.pdf]

Rosner, M., Joachimsen, J. (2012) *The Maltese Language in the Digital Age / Il-Lingwa Maltija Fl-Era Diġitali.* META-NET White Paper Series: Europe's Languages in the Digital Age. Springer, Heidelberg, New York, Dordrecht, London. [http://www.meta-net.eu/whitepapers/e-book/maltese.pdf]

Rosner, M., Borg, C. (2022) *D1.25: Report on the Maltese Language*. European Language Equality. [https://european-language-equality.eu/wp-content/uploads/2022/03/ELE___Deliverable_D1_25__Language_Report_Maltese_.pdf]

Skadiņa, I., Veisbergs, A., Vasiļjevs, A., Gornostaja, T., Keiša, I., Rudzīte, A. (2012) *The Latvian Language in the Digital Age / Latviešu valoda digitālajā laikmetā*. META-NET White Paper Series: Europe's Languages in the Digital Age. Springer, Heidelberg, New York, Dordrecht, London. [http://www.meta-net.eu/whitepapers/e-book/latvian.pdf]

Skadiņa, I., Auziņa, I., Valkovska, B., Grūzītis, N. (2022) *D1.22: Report on the Latvian Language*. European Language Equality. [https://european-language-equality.eu/wp-content/uploads/2022/03/ELE___Deliverable_D1_22__Language_Report_Latvian_.pdf]

Skadiņš, R., Pinnis, M., Vasiļevskis, A., Vasiļjevs, A., Šics, V., Rozis, R., & Lagzdiņš, A. (2020). Language Technology Platform for Public Administration. In *Human Language Technologies–The Baltic Perspective* (pp. 182-190). IOS Press.

Tadić, M., Brozović-Rončević, D., Kapetanović, A. (2012). *Hrvatski Jezik u Digitalnom Dobu – The Croatian Language in the Digital Age*. META-NET White Paper Series: Europe's Languages in the Digital Age. Springer, Heidelberg, New York, Dordrecht, London. [http://www.meta- net.eu/whitepapers/ volumes/Croatian].

Tadić, M. (2022) *D1.7: Report on the Croatian Language. European Language Equality*. [https://european-language-equality.eu/wp-content/uploads/2022/03/ELE___Deliverable_D1_7__Language_Report_Croatian_.pdf]

Proceedings of the TDLE Workshop @LREC2022, pages 52–61
Marseille, 20 June 2022

The *Nós* Project: Opening routes for the Galician language in the field of language technologies

Iria de-Dios-Flores[1], Carmen Magariños[2], Adina Ioana Vladu[2], John E. Ortega[1], José Ramom Pichel[1], Marcos Garcia[1], Pablo Gamallo[1], Elisa Fernández Rei[2], Alberto Bugarín[1], Manuel González González[2], Senén Barro[1], Xosé Luis Regueira[2]
[1]Centro Singular de Investigación en Tecnoloxías Intelixentes (CiTIUS), [2]Instituto da Lingua Galega (ILG)
Universidade de Santiago de Compostela
{iria.dedios, mariadelcarmen.magarinos, adina.vladu, john.ortega, jramom.pichel, marcos.garcia.gonzalez, pablo.gamallo, elisa.fernandez, alberto.bugarin.diz, manuel.gonzalez.gonzalez, senen.barro, xoseluis.regueira}@usc.gal

Abstract

The development of language technologies (LTs) such as machine translation, text analytics, and dialogue systems is essential in the current digital society, culture and economy. These LTs, widely supported in languages in high demand worldwide, such as English, are also necessary for smaller and less economically powerful languages, as they are a driving force in the democratization of the communities that use them due to their great social and cultural impact. As an example, dialogue systems allow us to communicate with machines in our own language; machine translation increases access to contents in different languages, thus facilitating intercultural relations; and text-to-speech and speech-to-text systems broaden different categories of users' access to technology. In the case of Galician (co-official language, together with Spanish, in the autonomous region of Galicia, located in northwestern Spain), incorporating the language into state-of-the-art AI applications can not only significantly favor its prestige (a decisive factor in language normalization), but also guarantee citizens' language rights, reduce social inequality, and narrow the digital divide. This is the main motivation behind the *Nós* Project (*Proxecto Nós*), which aims to have a significant contribution to the development of LTs in Galician (currently considered a low-resource language) by providing openly licensed resources, tools, and demonstrators in the area of intelligent technologies.

Keywords: Language technologies, Galician, linguistic rights, low-resource languages.

1. Introduction

Proxecto Nós[1] (The *Nós* Project) is an initiative promoted by the Galician Government (Xunta de Galicia), aimed at providing the Galician language (co-official language, together with Spanish, in the autonomous region of Galicia, located in northwestern Spain) with openly licensed resources, tools, demonstrators and use cases in the area of intelligent language technologies. The execution of *Proxecto Nós* has been entrusted to the University of Santiago de Compostela and is currently being carried out by a research team comprising members of the Instituto da Lingua Galega (ILG) and the Centro Singular de Investigación en Tecnoloxías Intelixentes (CiTIUS). *Nós* was planned as an ambitious initiative aimed to attract over €15 million in European funding. This paper presents the overall objectives taking this funding into account. Currently, the project is funded through a yearly agreement between the Galician Government and the University of Santiago de Compostela. This led to adopting a narrower focus for the Project's beginning (2021-2022), whose initial planning and documentation phase started in the last trimester of 2021 and ended in the first trimester of the current year.

The first stage of *Nós*, spanning from 2021 to 2025, will lay the foundations and provide the resources that will help place Galician among the languages that realize their full potential in the digital society and economy. The resources, tools and applications created within the *Nós* Project will improve technological support for Galician in order to achieve full digital language equality for both the present and the future. The ultimate goal is that Galician, as a low-to-medium resource language, will have reached the state where it has the necessary digital resources available to prosper as what is known as a "living" language in the digital age (Gaspari et al., 2021).

In an effort to generate the technological support and situational context necessary for Galician to continue to exist and prosper as a living language in the digital age, *Proxecto Nós* has been set up to address several areas from the natural language processing (NLP) realm. Specifically, the project is organized into several sub-projects (jointly established by the Project's research team and Xunta de Galicia) where each sub-project corresponds to a major field from NLP. The eight subfields are the following: (i) speech synthesis, (ii) speech recognition, (iii) dialogue systems, (iv) error detection, (v) machine translation (MT), (vi) text generation, (vii) information extraction (IE), and (viii) opinion mining and fact checking. *Proxecto Nós* aims to address these eight sub-fields by first creating linguistic and computational resources in order to then build applications

[1]https://nos.gal/

based on these resources. Such applications will act as visible and accessible demonstrators of the technology developed in the Project and will, in turn, produce a tractor effect that will lead to the development of new products (use cases).

2. Background

2.1. Context and Motivation

The development of language technologies is a strategic innovation area geared towards augmenting the digital presence of a language in a society. It has been a priority in both Spanish (e.g. Plan Estatal de Investigación Científica y Técnica y de Innovación, Estrategia Española de Ciencia y Tecnología y de Innovación) and European scientific planning (e.g. Horizon 2020). Technologies such as MT, IE, text analytics, and conversational systems play a critical role in the digital society, culture, and economy.

Currently, linguistic data make up a very large part of the ever-increasing wealth of big data (Jill Evans et al., 2018). High-demand languages, such as English, benefit from a large amount of computational resources which can help to develop NLP software and tools. These languages benefit from a long-standing research tradition in different areas of language development, and their integration into artificial intelligence (AI) applications associated with the latest electronic devices such as conversational AI or automatic dictation software is high. Several language projects receive governmental funding such as the variety of projects financed by DARPA. Other languages that have come later to the table of AI research, such as Chinese, are currently following in the footsteps of English. Projects for Chinese, like the one from Qian Yan at Baidu, offer significant improvements for this language.

For those languages that cover a smaller set of speakers and, thus, are in lower demand, there exist efforts from local governments and other agencies to increase their use. A few projects similar to *Nós* include AINA, which aims to develop digital and linguistic resources for Catalan, several projects carried out at the HiTZ Research Center for Basque, CorCenCC for Welsh in Great Britain, and UQAILAUT for Inuktitut in Canada.

The democratization of language technologies has a great social and cultural impact on the communities that use them (Ahmed and Wahed, 2020). For instance, MT increases access to contents in different languages, thus facilitating intercultural relations; dialogue systems allow us to communicate with machines in our own language; and semantic technologies enable advances in the automatic comprehension of texts, thus making it possible to process enormous quantities of documents. In the case of less-resourced languages such as Galician, the fact of incorporating the language into state-of-the-art AI applications can not only significantly favor its prestige (a decisive factor in language normalization), but also guarantee citizens' language rights, reduce social inequality, and narrow the digital divide (Jill Evans et al., 2018). Furthermore, the capacity to model language ensures a promising future for such technologies from both an economic and research and innovation perspective.

2.2. State of the Art: Galician Resources and Technologies

In 2012, work on Galician described a language with a level of technological support that "gives rise to cautious optimism". However, the authors also highlighted the need for creating new resources and tools for Galician, as well as directing more effort into LT (Language Technology) research, innovation, and development (García-Mateo and Arza, 2012).

In the last two decades, different research projects on Galician resulted in speech processing resources such as Cotovía(Rodríguez-Banga et al., 2012), the CORGA annotated reference corpus (Domínguez Noya et al., 2020) and other specialized corpora, both textual such as CLUVI (Gómez Guinovart, 2008), CTG (Gómez Guinovart, 2008), or TreeGal (García, 2016) and speech corpora like CORILGA (Regueira Fernández, 2012) and AGO (Rei, 2017). Furthermore, there are also functional morphosyntactic lemmatizers and taggers such as XIADA (Domínguez Noya, 2014), FreeLing (Gamallo and Garcia, 2013), and IXA-Pipes (Agerri et al., 2014), MT systems like GAIO (Xunta de Galicia, nd) or OpenTrad (Imaxin-Software, 2010), spellcheckers like OrtoGal (TALG, 2006 2019) and grammar checkers such as Avalingua (Gamallo et al., 2015). Also available are language analysis and information extraction tools like Linguakit (Gamallo et al., 2018) and language models such as SemantiGal (Garcia, 2021), Bertinho (Vilares et al., 2021), as well as other resources.

Furthermore, Galician is currently part of multilingual crowd-sourced data collection initiatives carried out by important companies on the global IT market, which have resulted in speech databases such as Google's SLR77 (Kjartansson et al., 2020) and Mozilla's Mozilla CommonVoice 7.0 and 8.0 (Ardila et al., 2020). This situation is reflected in a recent report on the current state of the LT field for Galician (Ramírez Sánchez and García Mateo, 2022), which informed on the considerable growth in the production of high-quality Galician resources and services, especially text resources. Despite the quality of these resources, it should be noted that not all are freely and publicly available for the development of LT.

The LT field has undergone profound changes over the last few years since the introduction of neural network systems. Generally, training models using these state-of-the-art technologies requires large quantities of data and has high energetic and computational costs, which continues to be a challenge for low-resource languages. However, as many recent studies show, end-to-end technologies and open-source multilingual pre-trained models created using large quantities of data from high-resource languages (Shen et al., 2018; Baevski et al., 2020; Wolf et al., 2020) can be used, through transfer learning and fine-tuning, to train models in low-resource languages such as Catalan (Külebi and Öktem, 2018; Külebi et al., 2020) or, in our case, Galician. To this end, the existence of resources and tools that are freely available to the scientific and business community is essential, and that constitutes one of the main objectives of *Proxecto Nós*.

2.3. The potential of the Galician–Portuguese connection

One of the main reasons that the Galician language is excluded from several technological efforts is the lack of digital resources. As an under-resourced language (low-to-medium resources available), a large part of the effort that the *Nós* project will be dedicating its resources to is the compilation of corpora and other linguistic resources necessary for the development of computational models and algorithms. One advantage, however, that Galician has over other under-resourced languages is its close syntactic, semantic and orthographic similarity to Portuguese (Pichel et al., 2021), a high-resource language. Indeed, Galician and Portuguese are two closely-related members of the same language family (i.e. Galician-Portuguese).

In order to get an idea of the sheer amount of text resources available in Portuguese compared to Galician we can look at the amount of pages available for both languages on Wikipedia as an index of the online positioning of languages (a metric used by some companies like Google). There are more than a million pages in Portuguese while in Galician there are only 176.681 (Wikistats, 2022). Moreover, Portuguese not only has a large amount of text resources available but it also has a large scientific community involvement resulting in a large number of NLP tools.

The proximity between Galician and Portuguese is an advantage of incalculable value that puts us in a very good starting position, since the adaptation to Galician of most of the existing resources for Portuguese would be relatively simple. This is something that different researchers of the *Nós* project have been empirically demonstrating by using Portuguese to improve Galician resources (Garcia and Gamallo, 2010) and MT systems (Malvar et al., 2010). Furthermore, the close Galician-Portuguese relationship has led to members of the *Nós* project being among the organizing chairs of the PROPOR conference on the processing of the Portuguese language, where works on Galician can already be published, being considered as one variety of the Portuguese language space (Pinheiro et al., 2022).

3. Project Description

The *Nós* Project has two broad scientific and technological objectives: (i) to integrate the Galician language into cutting-edge AI and language technologies, thus enabling its use in human-machine interactions; and (ii) to produce a qualitative leap forward in the development of language technologies for Galician. For this purpose, resources, tools, and applications will be developed and distributed under open licenses, which will allow them to be integrated into existing devices and services (such as smart speakers or conversational agents) and future technologies.

To this end, specific objectives directly related to some of the major NLP tasks have been established. Each of these technological objectives will be executed as separate sub-projects which will allow the parallel development of different tasks and an overall more effective organization. Nonetheless, a set of general objectives are shared by all the tasks. The general objectives are: (i) the compilation of high-quality linguistic resources; (ii) the elaboration of language and acoustic models (both general-purpose and task-specific models); and (iii) the development of applications based on these models. In addition, the project will have a general coordination mechanism through which resources will be distributed and shared among the different subprojects.

The resources and models developed for each task will be made available to the public using common dissemination repositories (e.g. GitHub, Hugging Face) and platforms (e.g. European Language Grid) , thus allowing their use in all kinds of applications, services, and products, by the scientific community, companies, institutions, and society in general. The results will be disseminated through a repository available at the project's web portal (which can be hosted on internal servers), as well as other established and internationally recognized repositories. Finally, the project contemplates the complete development of applications based on these resources which will act as visible and accessible demonstrators of the developed technology and will produce a tractor effect that will lead to the creation of new products.

The general objectives, sub-projects and coordination strategy are further detailed in sections 4, 5 and 6, respectively.

4. General Objectives

The main objectives are described in further detail below:

- **Compilation and creation of linguistic resources.** In order to place the Galician language on equal terms with other languages in the digital sphere, it is an essential requirement to have a wide variety and large number of high-quality language resources (annotated reference corpora, web-scale corpora, task- and domain-specific corpora, parallel corpora, knowledge bases, dictionaries, etc.) that allow the development of cutting-edge technologies for Galician. These resources will be mainly created from zero, depending on the needs of each task. In addition, all the generated resources will be distributed under free licences to encourage their extension, improvement, and exploitation by third parties.

- **Elaboration of language and acoustic models.** Besides providing the required linguistic resources, statistical and computational models will also be developed based on these resources, using different leading-edge techniques. Thus, both pre-trained general purpose models and models adapted to specific tasks and domains will be developed by applying state-of-the-art techniques, mainly neural network-based deep learning. As with the linguistic resources, these models will be made publicly available under free licences, allowing them to be freely used by companies, institutions and end users.

- **Development of applications.** Lastly, as final demonstrators of the project, a set of fully functional applications will be developed, which will showcase the potential of the elaborated models and resources. At this point, the project aims to build both specific demonstrators for each of the previously listed tasks, and applications that connect and integrate different technologies. These demonstrators, apart from illustrating the work carried out in the project, will also serve to foster the development of new products bringing together new technologies and the Galician language.

5. Subprojects

In what follows, we provide a summary of the specific objectives for each of the eight subprojects, including some brief technical details on the necessary linguistic and computational resources, the proposed demonstrators and possible use cases that could be developed by third parties. Given that the project is still in its initial stages, adjustments are expected to take place along its execution during the next years.

5.1. Speech Synthesis

The objective of this subproject is to provide the necessary means (resources and technologies) so that intelligent devices and systems can speak in Galician, as a first step towards an interaction with these devices in Galician at the same level as other languages such as English or Spanish. To this end, we will create public datasets that allow the development of state-of-the-art text-to-speech conversion systems, with the ability to produce synthetic speech with different identities, styles and emotions. These datasets will contain voice recordings obtained from phonetically balanced corpora, with their corresponding textual transcription. In addition to being distributed publicly, the data generated will be used to train different voice models, both speaker-dependent and average voice models (AVM). As demonstrators of this subproject, the following applications could be developed:

- **High quality text-to-speech (TTS) conversion system**, with the ability to produce synthetic speech with different speaker identities (possibility to choose gender, age, etc.), speaking styles (radio news, conversation, advertising speech, etc.) and emotional expressions (sadness, surprise, joy, etc.). Among the use cases of the text-to-speech conversion system, in addition to its integration in general-purpose applications (virtual assistants, dialogue systems, automatic translators, etc.), it is worth mentioning the possibility of incorporating it into applications for people with disabilities. For instance, screen readers and audio description systems for visually impaired people, or mobile TTS applications specially designed for people with speech disorders or impairments.

- **Web interface for obtaining personalized synthetic voices**, which would allow end-users to obtain a personalized speech synthesizer with their own voice. To obtain these personalized voices, users will have to record a small number of sentences that will be used to adapt a pre-trained AVM. The objective of this demonstrator would be to show the potential in terms of adaptability of the AVMs, trained from several voices. As possible use cases of this web interface, besides the possibility of integrating such voices in different devices (e.g. GPS), this interface could be used to create voice backups (Erro et al., 2015; Erro et al., 2014). This latter development would be particularly useful for people who suffer from some kind of pathology (e.g. people who have to undergo a surgery that involves the loss of voice) to preserve the ability to communicate with their own voice. This interface would also allow applying cross-lingual adaptation techniques (Magariños et al., 2019), with the aim of obtaining personalized synthetic voices in a different language from the user's original language. More specifically, these techniques would allow to obtain customized synthesizers with the user's voice in languages other than Galician (e.g. English, Spanish or Portuguese). As a direct application, these synthesizers would allow to customize speech-to-speech translation systems, so that the voice identity of the original speaker can be preserved in the translated speech.

5.2. Speech Recognition

Together with the previous subproject, the ultimate goal of the speech recognition subproject is to enable a complete oral interaction in Galician between users and intelligent devices. In order to achieve this goal, it will be necessary to generate and distribute publicly a large set of speech and text corpora, needed to train acoustic and language models, respectively. The proposal of potential demonstrators for this task is as follows:

- **General purpose automatic speech recognition (ASR) system**, able to perform across different domains. As use cases, one of the main applications of an ASR system is to provide a voice user interface for other systems such as virtual assistants, dialogue systems, web browsers or automatic translation systems. Moreover, one should not forget the possibilities offered by ASR systems in terms of voice commands for intelligent home devices (lighting control, thermostats, intruder alarms and all kinds of household appliances).

- **Automatic subtitling system.** As a use case, this system could be used to develop a real-time automatic subtitling tool for Galician newscasts.

- **Personalized automatic dictation system.** The possible use cases of this demonstrator are its integration in office software (document writing) or mail servers (e-mail writing). Another interesting application would be note-taking during medical consultations. This system would allow capturing patient diagnosis notes automatically, reducing the average duration of consultations.

5.3. Dialogue Systems

The main objective of this subproject is to provide guides and packages of specific technological and linguistic resources that facilitate the construction of competent conversational agents in Galician. In order for conversational agents to be linguistically and socially competent, they must be provided with additional mechanisms that allow them to handle conversational contexts that go beyond the specific task or scope of use of the conversation. In addition to a refinement of conversation tracking techniques, we will combine machine learning with knowledge representation (e.g. semantic networks and graphs) to reduce the amount of linguistic data needed and take advantage of existing resources from other languages. This is especially important in the context of Galician, which lacks a large annotated corpus to be used in dialogue systems.
As demonstrator of this subproject, we plan to develop the following application:

- **Chatbot-like conversational agent** to focus the interaction on the input and output of text in Galician. Among the most interesting use cases we highlight the specialization of the conversational agent for task-oriented application domains, for example the management of citizen appointments for the public administration, and for a more general scope (tourism, integration of cultural information, etc.).

5.4. Automatic Error Detection

The linguistic correction and evaluation subproject aims to provide the Galician language with a series of improved applications which make it possible to verify, correct and evaluate texts automatically at different levels using natural language processing techniques to detect and classify errors or deviations. To achieve this goal, we will design computer programs for spelling, grammar and style correction based on already existing tools adapted to Galician (e.g. Galgo by imaxin|software and Xunta de Galicia or Avalingua-CiTIUS). These tools will be improved with the most advanced techniques so that the identification of errors regarding words in context (spelling correction) and sequences of words and structures (grammatical correction) reaches the state of the art for major languages. Thus, we will not limit ourselves to the identification of errors, but also on the use of appropriate or preferred linguistic structures, lexical-semantic content and density, and the coherence and fluency of a text. For the latter, it is necessary to have libraries and linguistic and computational resources of greater complexity, which can represent the semantic content by grouping words and categorize texts using statistical methods or through automatic learning based on texts labeled by expert evaluators. As possible demonstrators of this subproject, we plan to develop the following online applications (which would be integrated in a single tool):

- **Spelling, grammar and style proofreader of texts.**

- **Linguistic quality evaluator.**

- **Tone and sensitivity analyzer.**

These applications would provide the Galician language with a series of valuable resources to improve the quality of the written language in all areas (education, press, private sector, etc.). In addition, they could be added to different programs or contexts through use cases adapted by third parties (browsers, email managers, office software, intelligent keyboards in mobile phones/tablets, etc.). For example, as a domain-specific use case, they could be adapted for the automatic evaluation of the linguistic quality of the works elaborated by high school and university students, of the entries in Galipedia, or even in order to adapt past literary resources to the current Galician standard. Another socially relevant use case is a correction/management system that promotes inclusive language.

5.5. Machine Translation

The MT subproject consists of the development of neural translation systems that allow both native speakers of Galician and professional companies and institutions to translate texts and short documents quickly and accurately. At present, there are different automatic translation systems with a linguistic rule-based approach, such as the open source automatic translation service platform Opentrad of the company imaxin—software, which is implemented and improved in the automatic translator Gaio of Xunta de Galicia (AMTEGA). However, there are no state-of-the-art models based on neural AI techniques with a web interface for high quality translations in Galician.

Our proposal includes the development of the whole End-to-End system that consists of the research, implementation and testing of an on-line MT system that will compete with other MT systems of similar strategies as those provided by companies, such as Google, Microsoft, and Yandex, where Galician is offered as a source language to be translated, but the quality of translation is not yet at the level of the languages with more resources. The improvement of translation will be achieved by taking advantage of the highest quality models that will be created within the *Nós* project.

The proposal of demonstrators for this subproject is as follows:

- **NMT translator from Galician to other languages and vice versa.** The defined strategic language pairs are Galician-Spanish, Galician-Portuguese and Galician-English, although other pairs could be incorporated later on. As use cases, these general translating systems, including the linguistic resources used for their implementation, could be adapted for specific domains by third parties.

5.6. Text Generation

The main objective of this subproject is to focus on the development of computational and linguistic resources for the automatic natural language generation (NLG) of texts in Galician language. The focus is on data-to-text resources, since most of the resources of interest in the text-to-text area are already dealt with in other subprojects. We will address the two existing approaches for this type of systems: the traditional template-based approach and more recent end-to-end approaches based on different deep learning artificial neural network architectures. Both approaches present major scientific and technological challenges and require the development of computational and linguistic resources for the construction of impactful systems and applications. One of these challenges is the reliability of validation by automatic metrics of neural end-to-end systems, especially in critical applications. Thus, it will be necessary to design strategies to contrast and verify the texts generated by data-to-text neural systems with respect to the original data and to develop the necessary technology that facilitates this verification in a semi-automated way. A critical aspect when defining demonstrators in the NLG environment is their ability to transmit information to visually impaired people, when combined with text-to-speech systems, as well as to overcome the limitations of small display devices (mobiles, tablets, etc.) where graphical visualization is not suitable.

The demonstrators that we aim for in this area are:

- **Automatic generator of different types of visualization graphs** (time series, bar charts, trend charts, etc.) of a generic type, which are commonly used in all types of reports.

- **Automatic real-time data report generator**, with direct application in the industrial sector (ICT, production or industrial plants, logistics, etc.).

- **Abstractive summarizer** of a general type based on end-to-end models.

The technology developed for these demonstrators can prompt impactful use cases such as the automatic generator of weather forecasts and environmental information, the automatic generator of medical reports from the data available in the medical history, an automatic generator of banking or personal economy reports or an automatic generator of informative chronicles, among many others.

5.7. Information Extraction

This subproject will focus on developing a set of text-to-data techniques for discovering and extracting relevant and salient knowledge from large amounts of unstructured Galician text. Its main goal is to extract knowledge elements or regular patterns from a collection of documents, especially content extracted from the web and social media. Since the extraction task is a very broad set of techniques, before going into the description of the specific demonstrators, it is necessary to define several empirical challenges such as (i) semantic relation extraction, (ii) named entity recognition (NER), (iii) entity linking, (iv) event detection, (v) topic modelling for unsupervised document classification, or (vi) keyword and terminology extraction. Once these information extraction techniques have been dealt with, some examples of possible demonstrators that we plan to develop are:

- **Question answering system (QA) of encyclopedic character**. A QA system mainly based on unsupervised learning needs NER and relation extraction techniques to structure the information from a source corpus (e.g. Galician Wikipedia), and thus be able to map the question with the extracted information and candidate to be the most successful answer. The development of this system also involves the semi-automatic construction of a knowledge base or ontology where the extracted information is organized.

- **Semantic annotating tool with linked data** for the creation of teaching materials in Galician: By means of NER and entity linking, we proceed to the enrichment of teaching materials in Galician. For example, new information can be added to the terms and entities identified in a text by linking them to the corresponding entries in the Galician Wikipedia.

- **Document classifier.** This system can be applied to any collection of Galician documents to be organized and grouped into non-predefined clusters. For this demonstrator, it will be necessary to take into account terminology extraction and topic modeling algorithms.
- **Extractive summarizer** that extracts relevant chunks from input documents to build summaries of different sizes, according to the users' needs. Extractive summarization techniques based on prior identification of relevant keywords and multiwords will be explored.

In addition to these demonstrators, the tools and models elaborated have the potential of giving rise to a wide variety of use cases from third parties, such as a process model generator from medical reports or a detector of depression signals in social networks, which would require most of the information extraction techniques developed in the scope of the project.

5.8. Opinion Mining and Fact Checking

This subproject will focus on providing the necessary resources and technologies to carry out basic opinion mining and fact checking analyses in Galician. To carry out the task of opinion mining, we will explore unsupervised strategies based on the use of polarized lexicons as well as supervised techniques dependent on annotated corpora with information about the polarity of the texts. Besides the generic models created with large corpora, it will be necessary to elaborate polarized lexicons using automatic and semi-automatic techniques, as well as to annotate new datasets with polarized texts. The classifiers created will take into account morphosyntactic and syntactic analysis to deal more correctly with complex linguistic phenomena such as negation and compositionality (Vilares et al., 2017). They will also take into account the information provided by a NER for the identification of entities mentioned in the text. This information is crucial in order to implement surveillance and monitoring systems on those entities, namely, products, companies, organizations, people, etc.

Regarding the verification or checking of factual information, we will distinguish, on the one hand, the process of extracting verifiable factual information (or facts) and, on the other hand, the process of verification of the factual content itself. For the first process, it is essential to consider factual information extraction tools, such as those derived from the extraction of open information, focused on the identification of basic propositions in the input text. It is also essential to have information resources where news and information contrasted in reliable sources and knowledge bases are compiled. For the checking process, we use textual semantic techniques focused on the computation of sentence similarity with neural networks and transformers. These techniques allow us to compare the sentences that convey factual information, extracted from the input texts, with truthful data previously contrasted in knowledge bases and reliable sources.

Taking the above into account, we consider building the following demonstrators:

- **Monitoring system of Galician products, companies and organizations.**
- **Map of the best-valued Galician locations in real time.**
- **Bilingual (Galician-Spanish) news checker.**
- **App focused on the identification of Galician toxic bots on Twitter.**

From the generic linguistic resources and language models used to implement these demonstrators, it will be possible to successfully develop use cases adapted to specific domains, such as, for example, a system for monitoring the products of a specific company, a map of top-rated Galician tourist sites, or a fact checker in the health domain specialized in detecting false rumors.

6. Project Management

The established scientific and technological objectives are organized into a set of work packages (WPs) whose interrelation is illustrated in Figure 1. Each of these WPs, briefly described below, comprises a series of tasks and deliverables that guarantee the fulfillment of the project's objectives:

- **WP1 – Global project management.** The goal of this work package is to ensure the effective coordination and management of the different subprojects as well as the overseeing of the deliverables, without forgetting the ethical and legal dimensions.
- **WP2 – Monitoring, evaluation, and continuous contribution to the state of the art of science and technology.** This work package comprises the development of a methodology for monitoring the state of the art of all the tasks involved in the project. This will allow the design of an experimentation plan suitable for each of the subprojects, which will be developed in the work packages 3, 4 and 5. This design might be updated as the state of the art evolves.
- **WP3 – Obtaining and creating high-quality language resources.** The aim of this work package is to develop different types of high quality corpora (spoken and written) containing deep-annotated linguistic information. In general, three types of corpora will be needed: on the one hand, a reference corpus for Galician and a web macro-corpus, both to be used by all the subprojects; and, on the other hand, different purpose-specific corpora (datasets).

- **WP4 – Construction and evaluation of state-of-the-art language and acoustic models.** This package will focus on the development of different models for all the subprojects and tasks (language models, acoustic models, etc.) from the resources obtained in package 3. This will involve the use of different linguistic tools (either adapted or created from zero) and state-of-the-art deep learning techniques.
- **WP5 – Development and evaluation of demonstrators and use cases.** The purpose of this package is the development of the agreed set of demonstrators and use cases, as well as the methodologies and systems necessary for their proper evaluation, whether perceptual or automatic. To this end, both objective and perceptual performance measures will be used.
- **WP6 – Publication and dissemination.** This package includes the publication of the project's outcomes (models, tools, demonstrators and use cases) for their general use, the divulgation of scientific results (publication in specialized journals and conference proceedings), as well as the launch of different calls for interest. It also envisages the development of an online repository that will allow not only testing the different demonstrators, but also freely downloading all the resources and the associated source code.

The central workflow of the project encompasses work packages 3, 4 and 5. These packages are the cornerstone of the project since they focus on the most relevant scientific and technological tasks: the development of linguistic resources, language and acoustic models and demonstrators.

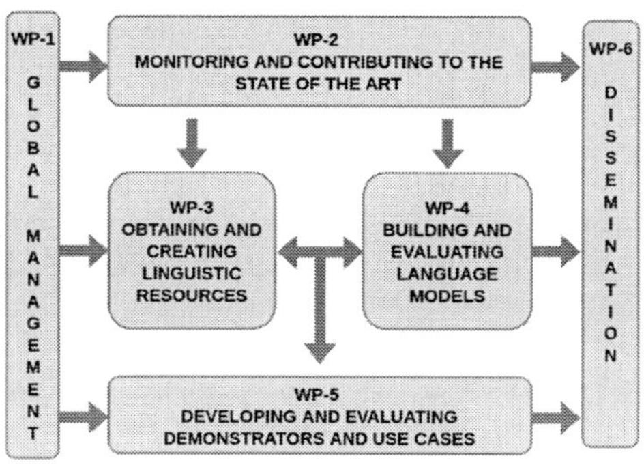

Figure 1: Interrelation among the different work packages that make up the project.

7. Current Developments and Future Work

Among the initial results of the project, we can highlight the first crawl of a web-based Galician corpus and a language model based on the CCNet tools and data (Ortega et al., 2022b), the development and testing of two BERT language models (with 12 and 6 layers, respectively) (Garcia, 2021), as well as the development and testing of a Spanish-Galician neural machine translation (NMT) system prototype (Ortega et al., 2022a). For the current year, *Proxecto Nós* aims to keep generating linguistic and computational resources to explore different subprojects. Specifically, work will be carried out on the design and recording of a high-quality speech corpus of sufficient size so as to allow the training of TTS state-of-the-art models. On the other hand, a speech corpus for ASR will be compiled. In addition, parallel Galician-Spanish, Galician-English, and Galician-Portuguese corpora will be compiled and used, together with existing multilingual corpora, for the development of NMT systems. Additionally, a web-scale Galician text corpus will be compiled, larger than the one already constructed, to be used in all the subprojects working with written text included in Nós. Based on these resources, new language models will be developed using different state-of-the-art techniques, as well as demonstrators or prototypes of a TTS system, translation system, and automatic text generator for Galician. At the same time, efforts will focus on extending and improving the first systems developed, and on validating the results obtained via the creation of high-quality gold standards.

8. Acknowledgements

This research was funded by the project "Nós: Galician in the society and economy of artificial intelligence" (Proxecto Nós: O galego na sociedade e economía da intelixencia artificial 2021-CP080), agreement between Xunta de Galicia and University of Santiago de Compostela, and grant ED431G2019/04 by the Galician Ministry of Education, University and Professional Training, and the European Regional Development Fund (ERDF/FEDER program).

9. Bibliographical References

Agerri, R., Bermudez, J., and Rigau, G. (2014). Ixa pipeline: Efficient and ready to use multilingual nlp tools. In *Proceedings of the 9th Language Resources and Evaluation Conference (LREC2014)*, pages 26–31.

Ahmed, N. M. and Wahed, M. (2020). The de-democratization of ai: Deep learning and the compute divide in artificial intelligence research. *ArXiv*, abs/2010.15581.

Ardila, R., Branson, M., Davis, K., Henretty, M., Kohler, M., Meyer, J., Morais, R., Saunders, L., Tyers, F. M., and Weber, G. (2020). Common voice: A massively-multilingual speech corpus. In *Proceedings of the 12th Conference on Language Resources and Evaluation (LREC 2020)*, pages 4211–4215.

Domínguez Noya, E. M., López Martínez, M. S., and Barcala Rodríguez, F. M. (2020). *O Corpus de Referencia do Galego Actual (CORGA): composición, codificación, etiquetaxe e explotación.* Corpus y construcciones. Perspectivas hispánicas. Marta Blanco, Hella Olbertz and Victoria Vázquez Rozas (Series Editors). Universidade de Santiago de Compostela.

Domínguez Noya, E. M. (2014). Etiquetación y desambiguación automáticas en gallego: el sistema XIADA. 52:93–96.

Erro, D., Hernáez, I., Navas, E., Alonso, A., Arzelus, H., Jauk, I., Hy, N. Q., Magarinos, C., Pérez-Ramón, R., Sulır, M., et al. (2014). Zuretts: Online platform for obtaining personalized synthetic voices. *Proc. eNTERFACE*, 14.

Erro, D., Hernaez, I., Alonso, A., García-Lorenzo, D., Navas, E., Ye, J., Arzelus, H., Jauk, I., Hy, N. Q., Magariños, C., et al. (2015). Personalized synthetic voices for speaking impaired: Website and app. In *Sixteenth Annual Conference of the International Speech Communication Association.*

Gamallo, P. and Garcia, M. (2013). Freeling e treetagger: um estudo comparativo no âmbito do português. *Relatório técnico. Universidade de Santiago de Compostela.*

Gamallo, P., Garcia, M., del Río, I., and González López, I. (2015). *Avalingua: Natural language processing for automatic error detection.* John Benjamins.

Gamallo, P., García, M., Piñeiro, C., Martinez-Castaño, R., and Pichel, J. C. (2018). LinguaKit: A Big Data-Based Multilingual Tool for Linguistic Analysis and Information Extraction. In *2018 Fifth International Conference on Social Networks Analysis, Management and Security (SNAMS)*, pages 239–244.

Garcia, M. and Gamallo, P. (2010). Análise morfossintáctica para português europeu e galego: Problemas, soluções e avaliação. *Linguamática*, 2(2):59–67, Mai.

Garcia, M. (2021). Exploring the representation of word meanings in context: A case study on homonymy and synonymy. In *Proceedings of the 59th Annual Meeting of the Association for Computational Linguistics (ACL-IJCNLP)*, pages 3625–3640.

García-Mateo, C. and Arza, M. (2012). *O idioma galego na era dixital – The Galician Language in the Digital Age.* META-NET White Paper Series. Georg Rehm and Hans Uszkoreit (Series Editors). Springer.

García, M. (2016). Universal dependencies guidelines for the galician-treegal treebank. technical report. Technical report, LyS Group, Universidade da Coruña.

Gaspari, F., Way, A., Dunne, J., Rehm, G., Piperidis, S., and Giagkou, M. (2021). Digital language equality (preliminary definition). Technical report, European Language Equality (ELE) Consortium.

Gómez Guinovart, X. (2008). *A investigación en lexicografía e terminoloxía no Corpus Lingüístico da Universidade de Vigo (CLUVI) e no Corpus Técnico do Galego (CTG).* A lexicografía galega moderna. Recursos e perspectivas. González Seoane, Ernesto, Antón Santamarina and Xavier Varela Barreiro (eds.). Santiago de Compostela: Consello da Cultura Galega / Instituto da Lingua Galega.

Imaxin-Software. (2010). Opentrad: machine translation.

Jill Evans, rapporteur, C. o. C., Education (CULT), Committee on Industry, R., and (ITRE), E. (2018). Report on language equality in the digital age. Technical report, European Parliament, Strasbourg, France.

Kjartansson, O., Gutkin, A., Butryna, A., Demirsahin, I., and Rivera, C. (2020). Open-source high quality speech datasets for Basque, Catalan and Galician. In *Proceedings of the 1st Joint Workshop on Spoken Language Technologies for Under-resourced languages (SLTU) and Collaboration and Computing for Under-Resourced Languages (CCURL)*, pages 21–27, Marseille, France, May. European Language Resources association.

Külebi, B. and Öktem, A. (2018). Building an Open Source Automatic Speech Recognition System for Catalan. In *Proc. IberSPEECH 2018*, pages 25–29.

Külebi, B., Öktem, A., Peiró-Lilja, A., Pascual, S., and Farrús, M. (2020). CATOTRON — A Neural Text-to-Speech System in Catalan. In *Proc. Interspeech 2020*, pages 490–491.

Magariños, C., Erro, D., and Banga, E. R. (2019). Language-independent acoustic cloning of hts voices. *Computer Speech Language*, 55:168–186.

Malvar, P., Pichel, J. R., Senra, , Gamallo, P., and García, A. (2010). Vencendo a escassez de recursos computacionais. carvalho: Tradutor automático estatístico inglês-galego a partir do corpus paralelo europarl inglês-português. *Linguamática*, 2(2):31–38, Mai.

Ortega, J. E., de-Dios-Flores, I., Campos, J. R. P., and Gamallo, P. (2022a). A neural machine translation system for spanish to galician through portuguese transliteration. Demo presented at the 15th International Conference on Computational Processing of Portuguese (PROPOR 2022).

Ortega, J. E., de-Dios-Flores, I., Campos, J. R. P., and Gamallo, P. (2022b). Revisiting ccnet for quality measurements in galician. In Vládia Pinheiro, et al., editors, *Computational Processing of the Portuguese Language - 15th International Conference, PROPOR 2022, Fortaleza, Brazil, March 21-23, 2022, Proceedings*, volume 13208 of *Lecture Notes in Computer Science*, pages 407–412. Springer.

Pichel, J. R., Gamallo, P., Alegria, I., and Neves, M. (2021). A methodology to measure the diachronic language distance between three languages based on perplexity. *Journal of Quantitative Linguistics*, 28(4):306–336.

Vládia Pinheiro, et al., editors. (2022). *Computational*

Processing of the Portuguese Language: 15th International Conference, PROPOR 2022. Lecture Notes in Computer Science, Springer.

Ramírez Sánchez, J. and García Mateo, C. (2022). Report on the galician language (deliverable d1.15). Technical report, European Language Equality.

Regueira Fernández, X. L. (2012). *Corpus Oral Informatizado da Lingua Galega*. Santiago de Compostela, Universidade de Santiago.

Rei, F. F. (2017). O arquivo do galego oral: xénese e situación actual. In *Gallæcia: Estudos de lingüística portuguesa e galega*, pages 545–564. Universidade de Santiago de Compostela.

Rodríguez-Banga, E., García-Mateo, C., Méndez-Pazó, F., González-González, M., and Magariños, C. (2012). Cotovía: an open source TTS for Galician and Spanish. In *Proc. IberSPEECH 2012: VII Jornadas en Tecnología del Habla and III Iberian SLTech Workshop*, pages 308–315. RTTH and SIG-IL.

TALG, S. (2006-2019). Ortogal.

Vilares, D., Gómez-Rodríguez, C., and Alonso, M. A. (2017). Universal, unsupervised (rule-based), uncovered sentiment analysis. *Knowledge-Based Systems*, 118:45–55.

Vilares, D., Garcia, M., and Gómez-Rodríguez, C. (2021). Bertinho: Galician BERT Representations. *Procesamiento del Lenguaje Natural*, 66:13–26.

Wikistats. (2022). Anexo:wikipedias. *Wikipedia-Wikimedia Foundation*. Available online at `https://es.wikipedia.org/wiki/Anexo:Wikipedias`.

Xunta de Galicia, S. X. d. P. L. (n.d.). Gaio: Tradutor automático.

Author Index

Association for Computational Linguistics
209 N. Eighth Street
Stroudsburg, Pennsylvania 18360

CURRAN ASSOCIATES INC.
proceedings.com

ISBN 978-1-7138-6141-6

9 781713 861416

Second International Workshop on Automatic Translation for Signed and Spoken Languages (AT4SSL 2023)

Sign Language Parallel Data - Challenges, Solutions and Resolutions

Tampere, Finland
15 June 2023